IPL
an inside story

cricket & commerce

IPL

an inside story

cricket & commerce

ALAM SRINIVAS • TR VIVEK

LOTUS COLLECTION
ROLI BOOKS

Lotus Collection

© 2009/Alam Srinivas & TR Vivek

First published in India in 2009
The Lotus Collection
An imprint of
Roli Books Pvt. Ltd.
M-75, G.K. II Market, New Delhi 110 048
Phones: ++91 (011) 40682000
Fax: ++91 (011) 2921 7185
E-mail: info@rolibooks.com
Website: www.rolibooks.com
Also at Bangalore, Chennai, Jaipur, Kolkata,
Mumbai & Varanasi

Design: Supriya Saran

ISBN: 978-81-7436-711-2

Typeset in Bembo by Roli Books Pvt. Ltd.
and printed at Anubha Printers, Noida (UP)

To
Nandini, the four As and K

TR Vivek

•

To Tarak Sinha,
our coach who insisted on 'catching practice'
with cement steps behind us.
He said: If you fear the ball, it will bounce back
and hit you anyway.

Alam Srinivas

Contents

RAJASTHAN ROYALS

Owners: Emerging Media Group (a consortium comprising Manoj Badale, Lachlan Murdoch, Suresh Chellaram), Shilpa Shetty, Raj Kundra

Franchise Cost: $67 million

Current Valuation: $125 million

Icon Player: None

Star Cast: Shane Warne, Shane Watson, Graeme Smith

Most Expensive Player: Mohammad Kaif ($675,000)

Glam Power: Ila Arun, former state CM Vasundhara Raje

Sponsor: Puma

KINGS XI PUNJAB

Owners: Preity Zinta, Karan Paul (Apeejay Surrendra Group), Mohit Burman (Dabur Group), Ness Wadia (Bombay Dyeing)

Franchise Cost: $76 million

Current Valuation: NA

Icon Player: Yuvraj Singh

Star Cast: Brett Lee, James Hopes, Kumar Sangakkara

Most Expensive Player: Irfan Pathan ($925,000)

Glam Power: Preity Zinta, Daler Mehndi

Sponsors: Kotak Mahindra, Coca-Cola, Provogue, 9x, Spice

IPL 2009 • IPL 2009 • IPL 2009 • IPL 2009 • IPL 2009 • IPL 200

MUMBAI INDIANS

Owners: Reliance Industries Ltd, Anshu Jain (Head, Global Markets, Deutsche Bank)

Franchise Cost: $111.9 million

Current Valuation: $200 million

Icon Player: Sachin Tendulkar

Star Cast: JP Duminy, Harbhajan Singh, Sanath Jayasuriya

Most Expensive Player: Sanath Jayasuriya ($975,000)

Glam Power: Hrithik Roshan

Sponsors: Adidas, Mastercard, Pepsi, Kingfisher, Royal Stag

KOLKATA KNIGHT RIDERS

Owners: Shah Rukh Khan, Juhi Chawla, Jai Mehta

Franchise Cost: $75 million

Current Valuation: NA

Icon Player: Sourav Ganguly

Star Cast: Mashrafe Mortaza, David Hussey, Brendon McCullum

Most Expensive Player: Ishant Sharma ($950,000)

Glam Power: SRK, Juhi Chawla, Rani Mukherjee, Arjun Rampal

Sponsors: Nokia, Reebok, Belmonte, Tag Heuer, HDIL

CHENNAI SUPER KINGS

Owner: India Cements

Franchise Cost: $91 million

Current Valuation: NA

Icon Player: None

Star Cast: MS Dhoni, Mike Hussey, Mathew Hayden

Most Expensive Player: Andrew Flintoff ($1.55 million)

Glam Power: Tamil film star Vijay, 'Drums' Sivamani, K Srikkanth

Sponsors: Reebok, Aircel, Peter England, Coromandel King, Radio One

DELHI DAREDEVILS

Owner: GMR Group

Franchise Cost: $84 million

Current Valuation: NA

Icon Player: Virender Sehwag

Star Cast: Virender Sehwag, Glen McGrath

Most Expensive Player: Gautam Gambhir ($725,000)

Glam Power: Akshay Kumar

Sponsors: Hero Honda, Adidas, Coca-Cola, Religare, Kingfisher, Fever 104 FM

BANGALORE ROYAL CHALLENGERS

Owner: UB Group

Franchise Cost: $111.6 million

Current Valuation: NA

Icon Player: Rahul Dravid

Star Cast: Kevin Pietersen, Dale Steyn, Robin Uthappa

Most Expensive Player: Kevin Pietersen ($1.55 million)

Glam Power: Cheerleaders from Washington Redskins NFL team, Deepika Padukone, Katrina Kaif

Sponsors: Royal Challenge, Reebok

HYDERABAD DECCAN CHARGERS

Owner: Deccan Chronicle Holdings Ltd

Franchise Cost: $107 million

Current Valuation: NA

Icon Player: None

Star cast: Adam Gilchrist, Andrew Symonds

Most Expensive Player: Andrew Symonds ($1.35 million)

Glam Power: Hansika Motwani

Sponsor: Puma

It Just Wasn't Cricket

It was so Kafkaesque. Existential, since one man was working against all odds to shape his own destiny. It was almost anarchic as things changed every few moments for no apparent reason. Finally, it was satirical as characters furthered selfish interests instead of looking at the bigger issues – security and national interests. Add petty politics, over-sized egos and arrogance, confusion, chaos, and cricket to this mix and what you have is a media earthquake, whose shock waves were felt across the cricketing globe – from West Indies to South Africa, England to Australia, with the epicentre in India.

Lalit Modi, the Indian Premier League (IPL) commissioner, thrives in Kafkaesque and crisis situations. He had pulled off cricket's biggest and most expensive league, the IPL, within months in 2008. Therefore, he had no qualms to shift its venue for season two to South Africa within a month in 2009. Nothing seemed impossible for Modi. In fact, he kept a brave and smiling face throughout the controversy in March 2009.

However, it was the manner in which the key players, cricket observers and experts, fans and the country at large reacted that proved that IPL has, in many ways, become bigger than the nation. More importantly, Modi, aided by his mentor, Sharad Pawar, former president of the BCCI (Board for Control of Cricket in India), and powerful businessmen (like Reliance Industries' Mukesh Ambani, owner of one of the IPL's eight teams, Mumbai Indians), had the audacity to literally hold the country to ransom.

Once India announced the dates for general elections and especially after the frightening attack on Sri Lankan cricketers in Pakistan in March 2009, it should have been clear to everyone that holding the high-profile IPL tournament in April-May 2009 (when India went to polls) was fraught with security risks.

So, when BCCI initiated talks with the Centre about the IPL dates, the home ministry's response was that the league's second season should be held after the elections. This was despite the fact that some of the states, which had IPL city teams, were ready to hold the matches. According to BCCI insiders, no one said a complete 'No'; it was just a matter of which dates suited the Centre and the states.

In fact, Home Minister P Chidambaram wrote to the concerned states and set two pre-conditions: one that no central forces will be provided for cricket security and, two that the states have to first fulfil the security expectations of the Election Commission (EC) and its requirement of forces for holding the elections. The home minister was categorical that no state can shun the second condition.

Later, the Centre asked BCCI to shift IPL dates to May. When Rajiv Shukla, an MP and chairman of BCCI's Finance Committee, met Chidambaram, he found that the latter was 'not averse to the idea' of allowing IPL to begin in May, instead of 10 April as scheduled. But the BCCI was adamant that it wanted the league to start in April; it wasn't willing to consider the shift to May.

BCCI's reasons for refusal were simple. IPL has nearly 60 matches and the logistics for organizing them in just over three weeks was extremely difficult, if not impossible. Plus, a shortened tournament in terms of period would have affected eyeballs and television viewership as several matches would have to be squeezed on some days. This would have affected sponsorship and other revenues.

Instead, the BCCI went back to the home ministry with a revised schedule, where matches weren't to be held in any of the cities either on the poll or election results dates. Confident that lobbying by Pawar, whose party was part of the Congress-led ruling coalition, would force the issue in BCCI's favour, Modi announced on 6 March 2009 that things had been sorted out and IPL would go ahead with new dates. He added that the opening and closing dates would remain 10 April and 24 May, respectively.

What Modi didn't realize was despite the revision, the states had still to contend with critical security-related issues. In fact, according to the home ministry only three states' response to the changes in IPL dates was positive. Most of them, including Maharashtra and Andhra Pradesh, continued to be apprehensive. These sources added that it was wrong for Modi and BCCI to blame these two states for first saying yes and then do a turnaround. The states never gave a firm commitment for IPL.

By this stage, the entire issue was completely politicized. BCCI sources claimed that while the BJP-ruled states had agreed to hold IPL matches, it was the Congress-ruled ones (like Andhra Pradesh and Maharashtra) and other non-BJP ones (like West Bengal) that opposed them. It now quickly became a Congress versus BJP issue and acquired several political overtones.

Later, the chief minister of Gujarat, Narendra Modi (with no links to Lalit Modi) criticized Chidambaram and said his state had no problems in providing security for IPL. Senior BJP leader Arun Jaitley too got into the act, and a few other opposition leaders also hinted that India's refusal to host IPL was a shame for the country. Chidambaram retaliated by releasing a letter written by Gujarat DGP that stated that security was a concern for the state. He added that Jaitley had a 'penchant for exaggeration'. Jaitley quickly reacted with a gem: when Chidambaram was the finance minister, our investments were not safe; now that he is the home minister, the nation's security isn't safe.

Other Congressmen were quick to react to BJP's allegations to ensure that the IPL didn't become an election issue. Talking to *India Today*, Anand Sharma, minister of state for external affairs, said that IPL was a 'commercial game and not India's national tournament. We cannot trivialize Indian democracy'. Speaking to the same magazine, Kapil Sibal, minister for science and technology, retorted that the BJP seemed 'more concerned about cricket than the lives of ordinary people'.

Between these allegations and counter allegations conspiracy theories cropped up from nowhere. The best one was about why Maharashtra did an about-turn and decided against IPL. The decision was traced at one level to the tussle between the Congress Party and Sharad Pawar's NCP about sharing of seats for the forthcoming elections. Although both are coalition partners, the NCP wanted a higher seat allocation (or at least the same) than the Congress, compared to 2004, when NCP fought on lesser number of seats.

After a meeting between the two sides, which was attended by Maharashtra chief minister (a Congressman) Ashok Chavan, failed to arrive at a consensus, Chavan informed New Delhi. The almost-immediate reaction from the Congress headquarters was that the state should oppose IPL, which could prove to be a slap on Pawar's face and would force the NCP to fall in line. It's a different matter that finally the NCP did get less number of seats than Congress – and almost the same as in 2004.

There was another twist to the Maharashtra story. At a lower level, there was an ego clash between two of the state's DGPs. In March this year, the state appointed SS Virk as the new DGP. But after the dates were announced for the general elections, the EC had a problem.

During the assembly elections in Punjab in 2007, the EC had forced Virk to be removed from the post of DGP as there were criminal cases pending against him. This time too, the EC directed that he shouldn't be part of any election duties.

Maharashtra's defense that Virk had been cleared in most of the cases fell on deaf ears. Hence, the state had to appoint another DGP, Suprakash Chakravarty.

Obviously, Virk and Chakravarty played a one-upmanship game against each other. After his appointment, Chakravarty gave several recommendations regarding IPL to the state home ministry. While maintaining that there was no harm in holding IPL during election times, he insisted on several preconditions. One, since transporting cricket players from hotels to the stadium and back could pose a security threat he felt it would be better if the players stayed at BCCI's facilities. Therefore, he suggested that all the matches in Mumbai should be held at only one venue, Wankhede Stadium, instead of some at DY Patil Stadium in Nerul, Navi Mumbai as was originally finalized by the BCCI.

In addition, he talked of other issues such as bifurcating security between elections and IPL so that the security of VVIPs campaigning in Mumbai could be taken care of. And he wished that a separate *bandobast* should be made for the foreign cricketers coming to the city.

Once the Congress-NCP tussle for seats escalated, the Maharashtra chief minister used Chakravarty's recommendations as an 'excuse' to scuttle IPL in his state. However, BCCI and Congress' Rajiv Shukla maintained that there was no politics involved in the government's decision not to hold IPL. He didn't see any clash between the BCCI and the Centre on this issue.

So, how did IPL become an issue between the Congress and BJP?

Political insiders explained that the concern of the ruling coalition partners at that time was that if an incident occurred during IPL (and of course, during elections) for some reason or the other, it would dramatically affect the election results. The Opposition, mainly BJP, would make it an election issue and blame the ruling government for its inability to provide security to Indian and foreign cricketers. The voters might perceive the government as a weak one, unable to control militancy and terrorism.

In this context it is clear that only the Congress-ruled states would have been cagey of holding IPL matches, while BJP-ruled states would be more or less relaxed. The latter were probably hoping that something did happen during IPL, which they could use against the Congress.

There were also intelligence reports that Pakistan-based militant groups may become active during elections, and this would become a matter of greater concern if IPL was also held during the period. After the Lahore incident, where Sri Lankan cricketers were targeted, and Pakistan became a pariah state as far as international cricket was concerned, the Indian government felt that Pakistan-based groups might want the same to happen to India. Hence, they were likely to attack the cricketers during the IPL.

Obviously, neither the Congress-ruled states nor the Centre could afford any risk in such circumstances. For political survival and expediency, it had no option but to scuttle IPL in India.

There was speculation that even some of the franchise owners put pressure on Chidambaram to hold the IPL in India – and in April and May. Media reports said that Mukesh Ambani met the home minister to discuss the issue. However, BCCI officials claimed that this was all rubbish. 'I met Mukesh and he told me that he was not a fool to discuss IPL. He said he had other important matters to talk about to Chidambaram,' said one senior BCCI official.

On 22 March 2009, when Modi got to know that IPL couldn't be held in India, he went into a rage. But he was not the one to give up. He had turned his IPL dream into a reality in 2008; he was not going to allow security or other national interests to come in its way. IPL would be held, he decided, either in India or abroad. That's when the search began for an alternative international venue.

To Modi's credit, he finalized South Africa as a venue within days – with the matches to be played in six venues from 18 April to 24 May 2009. But it wasn't easy; more important, the entire episode seemed hilarious. For example, when Modi was leaving for South Africa on the night of 24 March, a television journalist told him that Cricket South Africa hadn't received any intimation about his arrival. His immediate answer: they knew it two minutes ago. Actually he called them just 30 minutes before boarding the flight and they agreed to meet him after he landed the next morning at 5.30 a.m.

Initially, Modi had to choose between England and South Africa. Explained a BCCI insider: 'West Indies, Australia and New Zealand were too far away. Other countries in the subcontinent, like Bangladesh and Sri Lanka, had the same security concerns. We considered Dubai but found that the city would be hosting the Australia-Pakistan ODI series in April and, hence, its sports complex was blocked.'

Most of the franchise owners and Indian cricketers wanted IPL to happen in England. For the latter, it would provide an ideal opportunity to get match practice in England, which was also hosting the next T20 World Cup in June 2009. The franchisees thought of several commercial advantages of playing in England.

There is a huge Asian (including Indians) population in England, which could have been willing viewers and buyers of tickets. Several lakh Indians also visit England in summers, and many of them would have wanted to watch the matches at Lords or Oval. Therefore, they could create the same atmosphere in England, what they successfully did for IPL's season one in India. In addition, England is well connected with India as far as flights were concerned; even the various cricket venues in England were not too far away from each other and teams could easily travel by road.

Compared to England, the travel costs in South Africa were higher; there was only one flight to South Africa. Since the cities were spread out, there were logistic problems. Moreover, the cricket season had ended in South Africa, and they weren't sure about the state of the pitches.

However, Modi's first preference was South Africa for purely commercial and egoistical reasons. Many of the English Counties, which would hold IPL matches, were asking for too much money, plus the staying costs in England were much higher than in South Africa. In April, the weather in England is bad and Modi felt that nearly 70 per cent of the matches would be affected by rains. That, in turn, would have affected sponsorship, advertising, and gate receipt revenues.

There were telecast issues too. England and Wales Cricket Board (ECB) has recently given domestic rights for international matches to Sky Sports, which is at loggerheads with Setanta that has the exclusive rights to air IPL matches in England. Lately, Setanta had hurled corruption and other charges on ECB for giving the cricket rights contract to Sky, which was obviously concerned about the viewership for the England-West Indies series in England that would have clashed with IPL dates. Therefore, commercial rivalry would have played its role in Modi's decision to approach South Africa first.

We shouldn't also forget the ego clash between Modi and ECB/ICC (International Cricket Council). The chairman of ICC, David Morgan, is an Englishman who has had several issues with Modi in the past. Modi and BCCI have run roughshod over ICC several times in the recent past. Not to forget that the ICC is more concerned about the success of the T20 World Cup scheduled to be held in England in June 2009. Therefore, for Modi, England was always the last choice.

Finally, South Africa welcomed Modi with open arms. And the issue was settled – for now. But the dust didn't settle down, as there were several business and commercial problems. From the IPL organizers' perspective, they were unsure whether the second season would be as big a hit as the first one. 'BCCI is basically keeping its fingers crossed. It is waiting and watching. No one knows what will happen in April,' said someone close to Modi. More importantly, there was the huge financial angle.

'The coffers of BCCI will get hit. This is because the BCCI has assured all the franchise owners that whatever extra costs they incur – related to travel, stay and other administrative costs – and whatever losses they incur – on ticket receipts and sponsorships – will be compensated by the board. The overall hit on BCCI due to these reasons will be $20-30 million this year. In comparison, the franchisees will only gain,' revealed a BCCI official.

In the end, as IPL's first season as well as the two auctions (2008 and 2009) for foreign players proved, IPL was not about cricket at all. It was definitely about commercial interests – of the players, franchise owners and the BCCI. It was about entertainment and glamour to grab eyeballs, viewership and in-stadium attendances, which, in turn had the money angle. It was about opportunities for young cricketers to grab the limelight – and also land lucrative contracts.

But, above everything was the king-size ego of Lalit Modi, who thought about nothing but the success of the tournament. Nothing, not the ICC or other powerful cricket boards, nor national and security interests, nor powerful politicians, could stop him or even slow him down. He was a bull who was out to destroy all the china in all the established sports, business and political institutions – in India and globally. Modi was a man possessed, the magic wand, which could make billions of dollars appear out of nowhere.

Unfortunately, 2009 also marked the decline of Modi. His loss in the presidential race for Rajasthan Cricket Association, the filing of criminal charges against him in Rajasthan, his rubbing certain politicians the wrong way, his constant battles with ICC and other cricket boards – all may combine to cut him down to size. Or maybe, Modi would prove to be an exception, whose juggernaut will keep rolling.

CRICKETING A(U)CTION

As the IPL entered its second season, it was clear that cricket had truly become a glitzy and glamorous affair, a total tamasha. Nothing proved this better than the second auction held to sell over fifty foreign players on 6 February 2009, just over two months before the start of IPL season two.

To begin with, the choice of the venue told a story of its own. Modi shifted the auction venue from the last year's stuffy and bureaucratic granite-and-wood interiors of Wankhede Stadium, the headquarters of the BCCI, to the more relaxed and luxuriant confines of the Fort Aguada beach resort in Goa. Once business was transacted, the wealthy franchise owners of the eight IPL city teams had the option to host lavish parties over the weekend.

Modi also ensured that this time the GQ (Glamour Quotient) of the auction went up dramatically. No, it wasn't just because the Bollywood trio – Juhi Chawla (part-owner of Kolkata Knight Riders), Preity Zinta (who owns Mohali's Kings XI Punjab jointly with Ness Wadia, a noted industrialist) and the latest 'Big Boss', Shilpa Shetty (who had recently taken a minority stake with boyfriend Raj Kundra in Jaipur's Rajasthan Royals) – turned out in designer outfits, carrying Louis Vuitton and Prada handbags, and sporting their seemingly-oversized Chanel, Gucci and Versace sunglasses.

Some of the business owners of the teams outdid the filmy pack. UB Group owner and the promoter of Bangalore's Royal Challengers Vijay Mallya's sartorial pick – a red Aloha shirt with banana leaves and purple flowers printed on it – was a bit too flashy by any showbiz standards. But the best part of the 'Event' was that it was aired live on television.

'The auction is part of the IPL spectacle. Showing it live not only adds to the excitement but also tells the fans of a team how keen the franchise owner was in getting their favourite players on board. When Bangladesh's (and now Kolkata Knight Riders') fast bowler Mashrafe Mortaza plays against Kings XI Punjab, which fiercely bid for him during this auction, there will be a new edge to the rivalry for the Mohali supporters. The storyline only gets better,' said a senior BCCI functionary and a member of IPL's governing council, who understands the nuances of television entertainment business.

Not surprisingly, fans, supporters, observers, and the newly enamoured audience of IPL's first season were glued to their television sets as several Englishmen, Australians, South Africans and Bangladeshis were put on the block. Owners hurried during the few ten-minute breaks so that they didn't miss out on photo-ops and interviews. Modi too got into the act; during one of the breaks, he appeared with Preity on his left and Shilpa on his right

– the sports entertainer surrounded by his showbiz counterparts.

The scenes at the auction were as theatrical and dramatic as in a spicy Hindi movie. More importantly, people watching it live that day realized that cricket, or at least IPL, was more about big bucks and big egos of the owners; it was about BQ (Business Quotient), GQ and EQ (Entertainment Quotient); and that it was a commentary on the changing socio-economic trends in today's society, where an unknown player could become rich-n-famous in no time and for no apparent reason.

Given the fact that the business of sports was given precedence over the security of the nation, it was not surprising that cricketers were not present at the 2009 auction, unlike the first one that was attended by Sourav Ganguly, former India captain who led the Kolkata Knight Riders, and Rahul Dravid, who captained Bangalore's Royal Challengers in IPL 2008. Maybe this was because Indian players were away on a tour to Sri Lanka. Maybe even the ones who were in India didn't want to be too closely associated with the business of sports – at least publicly.

Whatever the reasons, auction 2009 became the preserve of cricket administrators (one spotted Rajiv Shukla on the dais with Modi and others), flamboyant and conservative businessmen (Mallya and Nita Ambani, wife of Mukesh Ambani), glamorous stars and starlets, and managers of the respective city teams.

Another thing evident this time was that the owners were taking most of the cricketing decisions themselves after the first year fiascos with high-profile teams like Bangalore and Mumbai where the players were chosen by the captains of the respective teams – Bangalore's team was decided by Dravid and Mumbai's by Sachin Tendulkar, India's master batsman. And both the teams had suffered as the little-known 'David' (Rajasthan Royals) walked away with the IPL trophy in the first season.

But once owners get into the act in any sports, big egos and big bucks become overriding factors that sway critical decisions. Take a look at how Jean Paul Duminy, the young South African batsman who was instrumental in the team's historic win over

Australia in tests and ODI series a few weeks ago in 2008-09, got picked up for an astounding sum, although he had less than a year of international experience.

Duminy's auction started with a base price of $300,000, and within minutes Mumbai Indians and Delhi Daredevils were locked in a bidding war. Soon the asking price reached a whopping $750,000 and Delhi decided to opt out. Just when Nita Ambani thought she had the South African in her small handbag, Kolkata entered the race with a bid of $800,000. Mumbai, $850,000. Kolkata, $900,000. Mumbai, $950,000. At this point, Jeet Banerjee, a consultant with Knight Riders threw in the towel. The first 'big' catch of the day went to Nita's Mumbai Indians. With her nose and chin up in the air (which never came down throughout the auction), her eyes glazing at the unseen horizon (they never dropped once), Nita looked smugly content.

However, the best was yet to come. Days before the 2009 auction, N Srinivasan, owner of India Cements and Chennai Super Kings, had given enough hints that he was interested in Andrew Flintoff, the fascinating English all-rounder. It was only a question of how much would he be willing to spend on Flintoff. Since Chennai hadn't indulged in any off-season trading (of players between the eight teams) or purchases, it had its full quota of $2 million (the ceiling set by IPL for each team's expenditure on buying new players) to splurge.

As soon as Richard Madley, the British auctioneer, who also conducted the auction in 2008, announced Flintoff's name, there was an expected buzz in the room. One heard laughs and sniggers in the background. This was the 'big' fish. Participants knew this bidding would be huge. They wanted to know whether India's captain MS Dhoni's tag of $1.5 million would be surpassed this time.

Expectedly, Chennai started the bidding at the base price of $950,000. Until $1.25 million, it was a battle between Super Kings and Kings XI Punjab with each making incremental hikes. When Chennai's bid reached $1.25 million, Preity and her boyfriend and co-owner, Ness Wadia took a breather. They talked and exchanged notes. $1.35 million. There were smiles all around. The war was getting hotter by the second. And suddenly, there was a new bidder: Delhi, $1.4 million.

Promptly, Chennai chipped in with $1.45 million. Preity and Ness went into a huddle – yet again. The camera zoomed on to Nita Ambani who was enjoying every moment of this incongruous bidding. She possibly remembered how she was forced to pay over three times the base price for Duminy not too long ago. She understood what this set of owners were going through, realized why businessmen were willing to pay any price for their favourite players.

Just when it seemed to be a tripartite fight between Chennai, Mohali and Delhi, there was another surprise. Rajasthan Royals' Shilpa, the new glam girl in IPL, raised it to $1.5 million. Flintoff was now worth as much as Dhoni. People – both participants and viewers – held their breath. Can Flintoff be more valuable and expensive than the Indian captain-wicketkeeper?

Nobody had to wait too long. As Shilpa held back to see what happens, Preity and Ness talked, and others watched in silence, Chennai upped the bid to $1.55 million. A new record was set. Flintoff was soon to become the highest-paid player in IPL. Shilpa laughed nervously and expectantly. She knew she wouldn't bid higher. Maybe it was the excitement of the auction that led her to jump into the fray. After all, this was her first auction and she was in the midst of cricketing history being made. Or maybe she just wanted to know how it feels to bid for a player for $1.5 million. Or maybe we were again witnessing the huge chinks in the so-called Jaipur's grand strategy of bidding low for relatively unknown players.

No one – neither Shilpa nor Preity (who had also exhausted her budget) – had the nerve to take on Chennai at this stage. As the hammer went down on Flintoff, the hall erupted a with loud applause. Chennai now owned two of the most expensive players in IPL – Dhoni and Flintoff.

In contrast, the bidding of another Englishman, the tall and explosive Kevin Pietersen, was more subdued and sober. It was as if the sense of excitement had been sucked out of the hall. There was an almost pin-drop silence, except for a few gasps, as Pietersen's name was announced for the bidding.

Bangalore's Mallya, who had never hidden his interest in this aggressive and towering batsman, raised his placard showing his intent to buy him at the base price of $1.35 million. People clapped and looked at Mallya as if they were sure the Bangalore team would buy this player. Before the auction, there were rumours that no one would bid for Pietersen at such a high price and that too in times of slowdown. Experts felt that the IPL Committee had committed a blunder by imposing high base prices for some of the players. This was the acid test. If Pietersen could be sold, and at a higher price than Dhoni or Flintoff, it would imply that the valuations were impeccable.

However, soon after Bangalore's bid, it seemed that Modi & Co. had made a mistake. It was indeed shocking that there was no second offer for someone who's considered to be probably the best batsman in the world today. Seconds turned into minutes. It seemed like eternity, or that time had come to a standstill. Mallya seemed confident that he had got his batsman. The 'spirited' owner would get Pietersen without a contest. Mallya readied himself for Madley to strike his hammer.

But Madley wanted some excitement; he goaded others to come up with a counter offer. 'Who's next?' he asked initially. There was no response. Preity looked zapped with the price. She sat still. Madley piped in after what seemed like hours, though it was just a couple of minutes. 'Is there any advance?' Then all of a sudden, the excited and bubbly Shilpa got into the act. Jaipur, $1.4 million

Yet again, it seemed more like the new part-owner was unable to hold herself back. Or maybe her boyfriend, who was also present at the auction, and other co-owners were allowing her to have a bit of fun. Or maybe, Shilpa had told them earlier that she was willing to fund such expensive buys. Or that she purchased the stake in the Jaipur team only on the condition that they would get Flintoff or Pietersen, or at least try to. We would never get to know, but we can hazard a few guesses.

Bangalore now raised the bid to $1.45 million. Shilpa seemed on the edge of her seat. She raised her placard again – $1.5 million. Mallya was all smiles at $1.55 million. Pietersen was now as expensive as Flintoff.

For a moment, it looked as if he might cross his teammate's tag. But then, Shilpa backed out. The hammer went down. Mallya pumped his considerable forearms in the air to a round of hearty applause.

In interviews later in the day, Mallya explained that he would have gone to any extent to buy Pietersen. 'Yes I would have gone all the way. I was willing to spend much more, even if it meant $2 million for KP,' he said. Now, in the first season, Bangalore had struggled in all departments of the game. The team's openers had one of the poorest averages in IPL, and the middle order packed with Test maestros such as Dravid, Jacques Kallis (South Africa), and Shivnaraine Chanderpaul of West Indies wasn't the most fearsome line-up either. But Mallya and his cricket adviser Brijesh Patel, former India cricketer, were confident that the $1.55 million they paid for KP might be the cure for the team's ailments. In retrospect, despite the strategic justifications by the several team owners, it does seem that the purchase of players such as Pietersen, Flintoff and Duminy was largely driven by the owner's fascination and faith. It had little to do with cricket. Duminy, as mentioned earlier, is still a greenhorn; he still needs to prove his consistency. Flintoff and Pietersen will be available for only half of the second season due to their country's cricket itinerary. So, why buy them in such a hurry? Maybe they may have got them at a lower price given the fact that global recession isn't going to go away in months, or even years.

However, the owners had their rationale to explain their emotional decisions. Mallya later announced that Pietersen would be Bangalore's captain in the second season for the matches that he was available for. The first season showed that he was unhappy with Dravid; he was particularly peeved with the fact that Dravid chose players that seemed more like a part of a Test team, and not T20 club. He also thought that the former

English captain could provide that zing to his team, which finished a poor seventh last year. In Mallya's scheme of things, T20 is won by exceptional batting; this explains his trade to buy opener Robin Uthappa from Mumbai Indians in exchange for the now-star bowler Zaheer Khan before the 2009 auction.

Similarly, in the case of Flintoff, Chennai's Srinivasan's belief was that T20 format is best suited for all-rounders; therefore, he went for the Englishman aggressively. In addition, Flintoff adds to the bowling of the Super Kings, which has been the team's weak point. And the middle order comprising Dhoni, Flintoff and South African Albie Morkel, now seems like a dream line-up for this team.

Whatever may be the reasons they were bought at such high prices, the players were happy. Duminy's father said that his son was 'ecstatic' and he never dreamt that 'he was worth so much'. The player's former manager in South African league, James Adams felt that 'JP is a brilliant player; he is good off the front foot as well as back foot. Above all, he is a levelheaded player. He will click in T20.'

Despite this takeover of the buying process by the owners, whose decisions were not always logical, some of the teams displayed exceptional thinking while choosing their team members. They paid less, and got the kind of players the team wanted badly.

Delhi Daredevils seemed to have made a brace of smart buys with the England pair of Owais Shah and Paul Collingwood for $225,000 and $275,000, respectively. GMR Sports' chairman Srinivas Bommidala, chief selector TA Sekar and COO Amrit Mathur had done their homework well. 'Our overall strategy, even in the first season, was to pack the team with as multi-dimensional and attacking cricketers as possible. As the purchases we made during the off-season and at the auction picks show, our decisions were based purely on cricketing logic. David Warner (Australian opener), Shah and Collingwood give us the desired firepower, while the addition of Ashish Nehra strengthens our new ball attack,' explained Sekar.

In the same vein, Rajasthan Royals' purchase of a relatively unknown Tyron Henderson was tactical. For one, he fitted well into Shane Warne's (Rajasthan Royals' captain) team, which was packed with lesser stars who gave their total loyalty to the skipper and had complete faith in him. (At this stage it does seem odd why Shilpa bid such high amounts for both Flintoff and Pietersen in auction 2009, when the overall strategy of the Jaipur team has been to have not more than one or two stars.)

The big-hitting South African all-rounder, Henderson, who helped English County Middlesex to win its first local T20 championship, was the subject of a heated battle between the Rajasthan Royals and Hyderabad's Deccan Chargers. After twenty-three rounds of bidding and counter bidding, the thirty-four-year-old fetched a handsome $650,000 from Rajasthan Royals – a six-fold increase over his base price of $110,000.

Australian player Shaun Tait, the first to come up for grabs at the 2009 auction, was also bagged by Rajasthan Royals for $375,000 without too much interest from the other owners. With Pakistan's Sohail Tanvir, IPL's highest wicket taker, unavailable this season because of Indo-Pakistan tensions, Tait was seen as the new wicket-taking option for the last year's winners.

For many watchers, the higher price tags for younger players such as Duminy, Henderson and Tait, compared to the lower ones for seasoned cricketers such as Shah, Collingwood and others, provided an insight into another important facet of IPL. As was the case with the first season, IPL has certainly become the fast track to riches and success for many youngsters, who would have never thought that they could have become superstars in such a short time and in such an unexpected fashion.

On the contrary, it is surprising that many international stars had no takers in the IPL. This list includes names like Ramnaresh Sarwan of West Indies, Australians Stuart Clark and Brad Haddin, and South African Ashwell Prince. All these players have proved their worth time and again in the past few years. But they were not even a blip on the various franchise owners' radars. None of the team owners showed an iota of interest in these players.

Nothing epitomizes this trend better than what happened in the case of Mashrafe Mortaza during the auction in Goa. For some time before his name was picked up, a string of players went unsold. Actually they included ten of them, mostly unknown names with base prices ranging between $50,000 and $100,000. It seemed at that time, when only a handful of players remained to be picked, that the owners were bored. All the excitement had been taken out of the 2009 auction after Flintoff and Pietersen.

Then came IPL's biggest catch. Actually, after other famous Bangladesh cricketers like Mohammad Ashraful had been given the miss, many assumed that the same would happen to Mortaza. But that wasn't to be, although it did seem like that in the beginning.

For a long time, there was no bidder for Mortaza. As Madley prepared to strike him as 'unsold' and nearly made the announcement, Kolkata interjected. Jeet Banerjee put in the bid at the last possible nanosecond. Once the dust had settled down, it seemed like a part of a strategy. Kolkata thought that by entering late it would not attract attention from the other owners, and would get its prize at the lowest possible price. This is called the 'sneak strategy', the one to get your way while no one may be looking in your direction. But once the bid was put in, others woke up suddenly.

At the last possible instant, Mohali's Preity put in the counter bid. Kolkata went into a conference. Should it bid higher for someone it was hoping to get cheap? But it did. When Preity raised the price to $95,000, Juhi Chawla, who sat at the Kolkata Knight Riders table, was seen smiling. This was fun. At $110,000, Preity looked visibly tensed. This was going a bit out of control. Little did she know that this was just the beginning.

At the bid price of $130,000, Juhi looked at her colleagues and smiled nervously. Preity laughed loudly and looked back at the Kolkata table. Juhi seemed to be really getting excited by this round as she looked at the Mohali table, which was in serious conversation as the price reached $150,000. At this stage, Juhi was laughing almost uncontrollably. She didn't expect this one to go on for such a long time.

Kolkata, $160,000. Mohali, $170,000. Kolkata, $180,000. It was clearly Juhi versus Preity. At this stage, Juhi was constantly looking at the Mohali table, hoping to catch some indication of when Preity and her team would walk away from Mortaza.

The bidding got to many of the non-participants, especially the BCCI members who were sitting on the dais. One heard comments like 'it is possibly the longest-ever bidding in IPL'. Another one said that Mortaza had become the most expensive player from Bangladesh. The situation was getting amusing for the audience.

Mohali, $190,000. Preity bit her lower lip as she raised the placard to increase her bid by another $10,000. Kolkata, $200,000. Mohali, $210,000. When Preity raised the bid to $230,000 several seconds later, she smiled shyly and nervously. This was first of its kind bidding for any player. There was a lot of commotion and laughs. Madley too got into the act and repeated what the BCCI members had said before. He made it official that this was the longest bidding in IPL.

When Kolkata reached $240,000, Preity hiked it to $250,000. Kolkata, $260,000. Preity raised it again to $270,000 as she went into a serious discussion with Ness. Auctioneer Madley said there was too much time being taken by both the teams and they needed to hurry up with the bidding.

During the $300,000 phase, there was almost a rapid-fire round of bidding as both teams hiked their bids by an incremental $10,000 every few seconds. It seemed that both owners were desperate to catch this seemingly small fish. It was almost surreal after Pietersen and Flintoff had been purchased in an almost lazy and predictable fashion by Bangalore and Chennai, respectively.

As Kolkata hiked its bid to $400,000, the television on which we were watching the auction went on a blink as the electricity went off. We cursed and cursed again. This was possibly the best part of season two's auction. We prayed for the lights to come back again soon which, thankfully, it did.

Preity was heard saying loudly whether she can bid in decimal increments now, say $409,000 instead of $410,000. Nervousness was now visible on both tables. Even Madley could be heard sighing. He had never seen such intensity in any bidding. Someone from the crowd loudly said that possibly it's time for bids in higher increments of $15,000 or $25,000.

At $430,000, Kolkata was on the mobile. Even as Knight Riders' coach, John Buchanan, was talking on the phone, Banerjee hiked the bid to $440,000. It transpired later that Kolkata was on line with its majority owner, Shah Rukh Khan, who wasn't present at the auction. (SRK had indicated earlier that he won't be involved in the second season – he was present at every match that his team played last year – due to his hectic film shooting schedules.) Newspaper reports indicated that according to Buchanan, 'Shah Rukh was on the phone from Mumbai and his words were clear, "Don't let Preity buy him (Mortaza)".' It was yet another indicator of how owners were calling the cricketing shots.

Soon, Mohali too was on the mobile. Ness was obviously talking to team's Perth-based coach Tom Moody and/or CEO Neil Maxwell in Sydney. As Madley asked the bidders to hurry up, Preity interjected asking him for some time until Ness got the advice he sought. At another table, Shilpa seemed all engrossed. As she said later, this was her first auction and she was learning a lot.

$470,000. $480,000. Now Madley was again hastening the bidders. $490,000. $500,000. There were loud claps all around. An unknown player from Bangladesh was commanding such a price. Half a million dollars! It was unbelievable. Was this for real? Had the bidders gone mad?

Both bidders continued to be on the phone as they had to decide whether to go ahead or give up. Finally, one of the parties blinked. At $600,000, the bid put in by Kolkata, and after 35 minutes of intense bidding, Mohali gave up. Preity made a gesture of cutting her throat with her hand, indicating to Madley that this round was over. Kolkata had won.

Later, Kolkata justified their prized catch. According to sources in the Knight Riders camp, the presence of Mortaza in the team could bring immense popularity and fan following from cricket-crazy Bangladesh, a market hitherto unexplored by Indian firms. The rebellious ICL (Indian Champions League) tournament that introduced the Bangladeshi team Dhaka Warriors in its second season was learned to have found a large and loyal following in the neighbouring country. In addition, there are a number of Bangladeshis in West Bengal and across India. So, SRK had pre-decided that he wanted Mortaza at any cost.

As owners, coaches, and administrators came out of Taj Aguada, Modi tirelessly hopped from one 24-hour news network to the other, from one press briefing to another proudly proclaiming that IPL had defied the global recession. Everyone promptly latched on to Modi's quote of the day. 'IPL is recession proof. This year's IPL will be twice as big as last year's. The $10 million spent today shows the strength of the Indian economy,' he said confidently in his slightly lispy manner and an American accent that showed no signs of wearing off.

With hardly a cheerful story to report amidst the economic gloom and doom, the business news channels quickly cottoned on to his broad-brush commentary on the state of the economy as if he were the governor of India's central bank. This also showed how Modi was the new Indian hero only because he had successfully married money with sports.

The Indian Promoters' League

Barely 24-hours after yet another 'inflation Friday' (Indian government released weekly price rise figures on Fridays until August 2008) had passed, and when consumers were worried about rising food prices, India's minister for food and agriculture Sharadchandra Govindrao Pawar was getting ready for one of the several crowning moments in his four decade-long career in public administration. If sartorial changes were an indication, his preparation was earnest. Having bartered his usual politico attire, the starched, all-white khadi, for a crisply-creased white shirt and black trousers, he had a more business-like look, and could have easily passed for a veteran investment banker.

While kicking off the grand finalé of the IPL's first season at the DY Patil Stadium in the Mumbai's suburb of Nerul on 1 June 2008, Pawar made a darn good speech – one that would have made any media planner proud. 'Good evening Mumbai,' hollered an unusually boisterous Pawar to the loud cheers of the 50,000-strong captive audience. 'I am extremely proud that whatever we have seen over the last forty-four days is a product of India. Today's final match will be watched in 122 countries.'

He went on to add that during IPL's first season, families had spent more time together, had dinner together, while watching the wholesome entertainment that IPL was. It was the kind of language that media planners used in the past to describe the success of television serials like 'Kaun Banega Crorepati' (KBC) starring the Big B, Amitabh Bachchan. If Sir Martin Sorell, the global advertising guru had been listening in, he'd have surely penciled down Pawar as a missed talent.

Another IPL architect, Lalit Modi, sang the same notes and emphasized that the tournament's idea was a statement from India to the world. 'It is a global representation of India, and what the modern day India stands for and its successes,' he chipped in. It was Modi's summer; he could hardly put a foot wrong. He certainly didn't with his assessment of India and the country's newest showbiz package. Events during, and around, the showpiece 1 June 2008 finals, provided ample evidence to show why he was right, yet again.

At around 6 p.m. on the day of the finals, nearly 90 minutes before the start of the match, the football field adjoining the DY Patil Stadium offered the first bit of excitement for the spectators, who were streaming into their appointed stands. Those already inside rushed out on hearing the monotonous loud, helicopter drone. When the silver-grey Bell chopper with a bold green Reliance Industries logo touched down on the well-manicured pitch, to the loud cheers of 'Mumbai Indians, Mumbai Indians', the guessing game began.

As Nita Ambani and her three children got down, a buzz started within the crowd. Is Shah Rukh Khan, the Ambanis' latest friend in the chopper? Are Rahul Gandhi, Priyanka Gandhi and Sachin Tendulkar accompanying Nita? Is the guy with a streaked hairdo Gautam Singhania? And where's Mukesh? It's then that the unmistakable silhouette of Mukesh appeared. And India's first business family trudged towards VVIP boxes accosted by security guards dressed in black suits.

This was the New India. An India where the grotesque display of wealth by the IPL team owners and their army of celebrity friends was part of the entertainment package. The teeming thousands who watched the spectacle were also part of the new, young and aspirational India, whose appetite for intimate knowledge about the lives of the rich and famous was insatiable. Where else could this be more visible than during the finals of the IPL which, as Modi never tired of repeating, was the quintessential Indian product.

Watching Mukesh descend from the skies reminded one of Chelsea's new oligarch owner, Roman Abramovich, whose big money has changed the English Premier League (EPL) forever. Abramovich uses his personal helicopter to reach venues when his team travels out of London to play its matches. However, even the wealthiest man in the wealthiest sporting league in the world doesn't fly into London's Stamford Bridge Stadium, preferring instead to be a part of a bulletproof cavalcade of silver BMWs to watch a game there.

But even he wouldn't have been able to fathom what was on display that day at the DY Patil Stadium, which became the finals venue, midway through the IPL competition. The stadium in the suburb of Navi Mumbai was chosen over the city's traditional cricket den, Wankhede Stadium, once IPL recorded attendances that were way above expectations during the early matches. The Nerul stadium can hold 55,000 people, compared to 30,000 at the Wankhede in South Mumbai.

The stadium is part of the DY Patil Vidyanagar educational campus that offers every conceivable stream of higher education – from medicine to hotel management. The standout architectural feature of this ˙three-tiered stadium (designed by Hafeez Contractor, if you insist on trivia) is the spooky 50-odd iron T-rex neck-like structures peering into the ground. It also has chopper landing and parking facilities that may have tilted the scales in its favour.

On the day of the finals, Bollywood starlets, and item girls danced to homogenized *Bhangra* song sequences. Shamita Shetty, dressed in a Bharatanatyam costume representing the South, gyrated to racy numbers from Hindi movies like *Jab We*

Met. So did a few Kathakali dancers who accompanied her. Together, the dances and the music ostensibly captured the cultures of the country's different regions.

The loudest cheers were reserved for actor Salman Khan, who strolled onto the stage for what turned out to be a three-minute advertisement for the game show, 'Dus Ka Dum,' which he was then hosting for IPL's media partner, Sony Entertainment. Among the several on-field product placements, Salman was one. It was hard to make sense of the rest of the 'cultural' entertainment that followed; the Mumbai crowd seemed to have got its money's worth and no one realized the match had been delayed by over 20 minutes. 'It's very well to claim that you've put together a world class product, but a football match starting late at any of the big European leagues would have been unacceptable,' feels Harsha Bhogle, a sportscaster, and a consultant for Mumbai Indians.

However, the atmosphere in the stadium was electric, quite like what one would witness during an India-Pakistan game. The fact that the home team, Mumbai Indians, was not playing in the finals didn't seem to affect the spectators. There was a 'yellow' contingent of over 200 members of the Tamil Nadu Cricket Association (TNCA), who were specially flown in by the owner of one of the finalists, Chennai Super Kings; in addition, local Tamilians had turned up in sizable number to cheer for their 'home' team. The massive Gujarati section, which showed up, seemed to have problems deciding which team to support – one of the local boys, Parthiv Patel, was playing for Chennai, while three other lads – Yusuf Pathan, Munaf Patel and Ravindra Jadeja represented Rajasthan Royals.

Getting into the arena was as difficult and chaotic as is the case in any other international game. Irrespective of the additional seats, spectators couldn't help feeling like canned sardines. Even if one had paid a huge Rs 8,000 for a ticket, he/she had to park his/her butt on an uncomfortable plastic seat. The concrete cage, floodlights, a breezeless evening, along with Mumbai's sweltering heat made matters unbearable. For the spectators, the speeches could have ended earlier, the game could have begun sooner, but then they were in the midst of one of the most significant events in global cricketing history; more importantly, the game was being beamed live in 122 countries.

Anyway, in India, going to a stadium to watch an important match is not for the weak. From buying a ticket to surviving the heat, hunger, and bird-brained security arrangements (at Chennai's Chepauk Stadium, for instance, policemen wouldn't allow spectators wearing black shirts for an India-Pakistan match fearing that they might use them as protest flags), it is a supreme test of human endurance and courage. If you can walk out without a headache, irrespective of who won or lost, you probably had a good day.

At the Nerul stadium, where match organization was entrusted with the local franchise, the RIL-owned Mumbai Indians, and not the BCCI, the situation was the same. The lone McDonalds kiosk ran out of its overpriced supply minutes into the mid-innings break, while Pepsi, one of the official non-alcoholic beverage partners of IPL charged a 400 per cent premium on drinks and snacks. Even if you did manage to grab a Pepsi or a mineral water bottle after a mini scuffle at the stall, the overzealous stewards wouldn't allow bottles with the cap on because they thought that the harmless plastic lids could apparently be used as mini missiles.

Watching sports live at the venue is about enjoying the atmosphere and sharing the thrills, excitement and disappointment with thousands of strangers. It's about getting away from the over-analysis of television commentary, recreating that sublime straight drive in your mind without the aid of replays from twenty different camera angles, and sharing notes with the stranger sitting next to you. It's like watching the complete picture as opposed to a mere frame on television.

But Modi and Co. thought otherwise. At the finals, each time a Super Kings player hit a boundary or a six, the team's chief entertainer, drummer Sivamani, played his signature beat. Or the cheerleaders in yellow danced to the rather unimaginatively translated-from-Tamil team anthem 'Yeh hai Chennai, Chennai Super Kings, we are yellow jersey participants'. When it was the turn of the Rajasthan Royals to bat, their official brand ambassador, the Indi-pop singer Ila Arun, screamed the official team anthem, 'Halla Bol'. Now, there are forty guaranteed mid-overs, mini-breaks and an average of fifty boundaries in a T20 game. If spectators are assaulted by the same song-and-dance routine for more than 100 times in the course of a three-hour game, it can get a bit stale.

Going by the evidence of season one, IPL was a loud, chaotic, and in-your-face product that was at times inelegant, but often exciting. Most importantly, it had sold, and sold big time in the New India. Maybe, the ace media planner, Sharad Pawar should have added in his speech that nobody ever loses money on betting on cricket in India.

WHOSE IDEA WAS IT ANYWAY?
When a cricketing event becomes a success in India, almost everyone tends to claim ownership of the idea. The same happened in the case of IPL. While most BCCI functionaries readily credit IPL as the brainchild of Modi, there are other claimants to the provenance of IPL or similar ideas for a city-based cricket league in India. It depends on which version you wish to believe.

People close to the late Congress leader, Madhav Rao Scindia, from the royal family of Gwalior, contend that he had thought of an inter-city cricket league along the lines of the English football league, or at the least a more modern version of the English county cricket structure, that would attract the best players in the world. One career sports administrator, who owes his lucrative involvement with many Indian sports federations to Scindia, says that the latter had planned to make Gwalior the epicenter of the proposed league, and therefore had commissioned an expensive overhaul of the city's Captain Roop Singh Stadium in the mid 1990s.

Although the stadium was already an international venue, Scindia installed floodlights and spruced up the facilities to match global standards. He got the international sports marketing and management firm, IMG to prepare a blueprint for the league around 1996 – a claim not refuted by senior executives working for the company then. 'At that time, we were working on several concepts, including an idea similar to the Hong Kong Sixes (an annual tournament with a six-a-side format), or a league that could co-exist with the domestic structure,' says a former IMG hand. But the plan fell prey to the vagaries of BCCI's politics, and the turbulent course of Scindia's own political career when he resigned from the Congress party briefly.

Tracking events involving the BCCI – or the birth of the T20 idea in India – is like reading the Mahabharata. There is no dearth of sub-plots, and there are alternate versions and interpretations. The Scindia story too has a twist, and none other than Modi holds the centre stage in this one.

According to Amrit Mathur, the idea of an inter-city league that was floating around in the mid 1990s, and which was taken up by Scindia, was actually Modi's. Even in those days, the US-educated Modi, who was in awe of the commercial success of the NBA's basketball franchise model in America, wanted to replicate it in India. He was already thinking in terms of private ownership of teams, which would have a fair sprinkling of overseas stars.

Since he was not actively involved in cricket administration in those days, Modi sought the help of some of his friends such as Piyush Pandey and former Indian opener Arun Lal to take his idea forward. Pandey, who sports a Merv Hughes (former Australian cricketer)-like moustache, has been one of the most influential admen in the country for over two decades. His creative campaigns for brands such as Fevicol, Cadbury and the two-wheeler Luna are considered the gold standard in Indian advertising. Moreover, the current chairman of O&M, the ad agency, was an accomplished cricketer who played as a wicketkeeper for Rajasthan in Ranji Trophy.

Over a decade later, when the concept of IPL became a reality, Modi roped in Pandey to package the eight-city cricket league and create an international brand around it. Given their long-standing friendship, Pandey's O&M was also entrusted with the brand building exercise for both IPL and Rajasthan Royals. Pandey's singer sister Ila Arun is the brand ambassador for the Jaipur team. It's all about connections and networks.

Arun Lal's cricket network too ran far and wide as he was the head of the newly created Professional Cricketers' Association in the mid 1990s. His mandate during the Scindia days was to coax Indian and foreign players to cast their lot with the proposed league, and identify talented young domestic cricketers. Lal's job was to do what former England captain Tony Greig successfully accomplished for the rebel Kerry Packer's World Series in the 1980s. It was Greig who recruited star players in various countries to participate in the rebel Packer series, even at the expense of being banned from international cricket by their respective cricket boards.

Pandey and Lal, along with Mathur, prepared a project and feasibility report for an inter-city league in the 1990s, but the BCCI wasn't interested in it. A reluctant Jagmohan Dalmiya, then the BCCI chairman, cited an obscure rule that such a proposal can only come from a state cricket association, and not from private parties.

That's when Modi's friends approached Scindia, who was then the president of Madhya Pradesh Cricket Association (MPCA). As a well-respected politician and a seasoned cricket administrator who was open to new ideas, Modi had hoped that Scindia would buy the idea. According to Mathur, potential sponsors, a media partner and team owners were identified, and most of the players who would participate were contacted. Everyone was excited about the prospect of a high-paying cricket league.

Sources contend that established players such as Dravid and Venkatesh Prasad (former India fast bowler) met Scindia to discuss the idea, and were even paid an advance to sign up for the new league.

However, unlike the current T20 format, Scindia's inter-city league was to be a 50-overs game, played over four to six weeks in summers (which is cricket's off-season in India) at various new floodlit stadiums. 'We hadn't thought of player auctions, but we had decided to have a graded contract system,' said Mathur.

At that time, when Ranji players on an average made Rs 40,000 a year; the proposed league offered Rs 200,000 in annual contracts for playing a few weeks of cricket. It was as lucrative as IPL turned out to be, if one considers the purchasing power of the rupee. Sensing that private ownership of teams would significantly dilute its own importance, the BCCI threw a spanner and said 'no' to the participation of foreign players.

The BCCI's decision meant the end of the Scindia league, even before it began. A league without international stars didn't make any business sense for sponsors. Two years of Modi's hard work amounted to naught as BCCI played party pooper citing technicalities and archaic rules, rather than rejecting the idea outright. 'In a way, it was good because in hindsight the market was not ready for such an idea. The event was tiny compared to today's IPL,' explained Mathur.

However, Scindia and Modi are not the only contenders for mooting the idea of such a league. The owner of Delhi Daredevils, the GMR Group, said that it too had pushed for an IPL-like format for many years with the previous BCCI dispensation. Delhi Daredevils' managers recall how they had sent several proposals and made endless presentations to the former BCCI chairman, Dalmiya, but all these efforts were in vain.

Then there's Shailendra Singh, the promoter of the advertising, public relations and entertainment company, Percept, who had a similar story to tell as he sat in his central Mumbai second floor office that boasted of a tennis court. According to Singh, many of living greats in the sports world, such as Boris Becker, Edwin Moses, and Tendulkar were his personal friends, and no one understood the combination of cricket and entertainment better than him in India.

Having organized nearly 1,000 exhibition matches with well-known cricketers and celebrities, he claimed to possess the 'magic formula' for at least a decade. 'I have done every possible tamasha that can be done around the game of cricket. What's the big deal about people coming to watch IPL matches in choppers? I've landed several helicopters on the cricket field. I've organized a game between Sehwag XI and Hrithik Roshan (the Bollywood superstar) XI; as also a Salman Khan team playing against Tendulkar XI,' he said while slipping in the anecdote about how he nearly got India's opener, Virender Sehwag to nick his first ball, while bowling his nippy left arm seamers. The last time he checked with the speedgun, Singh, who is in his forties, could bowl at a brisk pace of 130 kmph-plus.

To Singh's credit, when business houses think of cricket-related marketing gimmicks, he's the one they usually turn to. Having close ties with the Sahara Group (Percept has been the group's ad agency for several years and has been managing content and programming for the entertainment channel, Sahara One), the lead sponsor of the Indian cricket team, helped Singh's ambitions. Singh's other gimmicks include matches like the one between Filmstars XI and Doctors XI to celebrate the World Anti-Tobacco Day. Once every four years when companies are desperate to whip up the ODI World Cup frenzy, they usually like to throw a gala send-off party for the Indian team. For instance, cricket bats as high as Delhi's Qutub Minar are taken around the country so that millions of fans can scribble their good wishes, and write prayers for a victorious homecoming for the team.

In such times, Singh's services are sought after to organize candyfloss, nostalgia cricket. The tried and tested formula is to have India's winning team of the 1983 World Cup play the current one leaving for the World Cup. Normally, the 1983 veterans lose, Kapil Dev, the captain of the victorious 1983 team, makes a 'best wishes' speech, the current team is garlanded as if it was embarking on a medieval, kingdom-conquering sortie. In the end, the corporate sponsors and Singh go back home happy.

If one had the slightest hint of disbelief, Singh pointed to photographic evidence, and there was no dearth of it. The wood-panelled walls of his room bore nearly 200 photographs of him in the company of illustrious cricketers at exhibition matches around the world. To dispel any further doubts, Singh asked his secretary to fetch videotapes of some of these matches. 'I have virtually camped outside Dalmiya's office in Kolkata, and would go there every fortnight with a proposal of a glam cricket league. But I got nothing out of him. He would neither say no, nor yes. He was like one of those lawyers, whose only intent is to get the hearing extended. His constant refrain was: "We'll do something about it". It was almost as if I was asking the BCCI to part with its family silver,' explained the self-styled impresario of showbiz cricket.

Even if the idea of an IPL-like league was staring everyone in the face, and if it was only the fault of the previous BCCI administration that prevented it from taking off, Messrs Pawar and Modi can still claim to have tucked into the goldmine. Especially since BCCI was the last amongst major cricketing bodies to recognize the power and potential of T20 cricket. Before India took part in the T20 World Cup, and emerged victorious, the country had played a solitary international game against South Africa. Even at the domestic level, a T20 competition was only incorporated recently.

If it wasn't for the rebel ICL, which was conceived by domestic media mogul Subhash Chandra and the chairman of the largest Indian media house Zee Network, IPL may well have never happened. Chandra announced the formation of his 'rebel' league in June 2007, and that put pressure on the BCCI to either respond with an official league of its own, or smoke the peace pipe with the rebel players.

Sources felt that Chandra decided on a league of his own as he was disgusted by the manner in which he was constantly edged out of telecast rights tenders by the BCCI. Despite having bid the maximum for various rights, he was turned down for some reason or the other. Finally, he took the bat in his own hands, roped in former cricketer Kapil Dev, and launched ICL. After the success of IPL – ICL's first season was a disaster in that respect – Chandra renewed efforts to effectively compete with Modi.

An article in *4Ps, Business and Marketing*, published before ICL's second season started, stated that the organizers planned to spend Rs 50 crore, or thrice the amount they spent in the first season, for a new marketing campaign. Like the IPL, ICL hoped to expand the bevy of Bollywood stars that dotted its matches. Shariq Patel, Sr VP (operations and marketing) ICL, told the magazine that 'we are in talks with a number of Bollywood stars. A lot of them are showing interest. But it's too early to name them.'

Taking advantage of the fact that ICL begins in October during the festive season in India, the organizers were busy roping in new advertisers in August and September 2008. Basabdatta Chowdhuri, CEO, Madison Media Plus told *4Ps* that 'there is an interest among marketers for ICL because there are no other important tournaments in the month of October.' Other experts added that advertisers may wish to opt for ICL as it would enable them to 'break the clutter during the festive season'.

However, the supporters of IPL felt that the league had nothing to do with ICL. Going back to the beginnings of IPL, 'Modi wanted to start an inter-city league in the 1990s. The idea was always there at the back of his mind. We have not plucked it out of thin air one fine morning,' explained the BCCI's droopy-eyed chief administrative officer, Ratnakar Shetty a chemistry teacher at Mumbai's Wilson College, who continues to be on long leave in order to pursue his passion for cricket administration. Retorts a member of the ICL faction: 'If that was the case, and Modi was determined to start a T20 league to raise the standards of Indian cricket, why was it not part of the Pawar group's election campaign for BCCI's presidentship?' The inference: IPL was launched only to stifle ICL.

Balu Nayar, the former CEO of IMG who was with the company when it did most of the initial spade work on IPL, said that someone close to Pawar suggested to IMG in February 2007 to get in touch with the BCCI to work on a plan to revitalize domestic cricket. Over time, this plan took the shape of IPL.

As you meet different set of people, you realize that the beginnings of IPL are steeped in ironies, anecdotes and unbelievable legends. One of them is that the new age greed-is-good form of a cricket league was born at the bastion of old world gentility that has resisted change and commercialization stubbornly. In a meeting over tea, on the sidelines of Wimbledon, which proudly proclaims its traditional tennis past, Modi, Nayar and Andrew Wildblood, the London-based Sr VP of IMG agreed that India's domestic cricket structure could be overhauled profitably given the country's insatiable appetite for the sport.

In a two-page proposal after the Wimbledon meeting, IMG suggested a city-based league instead of the traditional state or zonal matches. More importantly, it urged that private enterprises should own the teams, much like the US franchise sports model. A few months later, in September 2007, the BCCI held a meeting in Singapore with the heads of two of the other most influential national cricket bodies – Cricket South Africa and Cricket Australia – to discuss the commercial viability of IPL, and the creation of the Champions League, which is now scheduled for September 2009 and whose lion's share of profits would go to the three boards.

THE SEARCH FOR OWNERS

Nayar and the IMG team sent feelers to big investors to see if they were interested in participating in the process of privatization of Indian cricket. IMG hired the Mumbai-based direct marketing firm, Direxions to compile a list of 1,200 companies, high net-worth individuals, private-equity firms and sports associations across the world, which could potentially be interested in owning a slice of the proposed league. 'We wanted to tap into the egos of entrepreneurs and the sense of patriotism among rich expatriate Indians to get them interested in buying a franchise. There was tremendous enthusiasm among PE investors for sports properties around the world,' said Nayar.

In ten days, Direxions established contact with potential investors and sent them formal proposals. 'It looked like a wild goose chase talking to 1,200 people from the Middle East to

Southeast Asia. But in the absence of any precedents and financial benchmarks, the direct marketing exercise helped us to gauge the level of enthusiasm for the idea and arrive at some valuation and business model for IPL,' said Nayar.

As the rebel ICL signed several international cricketing stars, most of them who had retired or were clearly over the hill, there were rumours that leading domestic players such as Mohammad Kaif were considering big money moves to the unofficial league, which had been shunned by the BCCI. It was in this atmosphere that the Indian cricket board announced the launch of IPL with the blessings of the ICC (International Cricket Council), and the support of all members of the various national cricket bodies.

India's win in the T20 World Cup obviously put IPL on to the fast track. After Yuvraj Singh's six sixers in the Stuart Broad over during the India-England game at the T20 World Cup and Dhoni's team winning the tournament, the country was ready for a massive entertainer in the form of IPL.

In November 2007, BCCI hired a professional employee with a corporate managerial background for the first time in its history. Modi roped in Sundar Raman, the head of Mindshare, one of the largest media planning agencies in India and part of the WPP empire, to be the COO of IPL. Clearly, television revenues held the key to IPL's success and Raman's experience in this arena would prove to be a boon. Raman's move surprised many in the agency business. Chucking up the top job at one of the biggest media planning firms in a booming advertising market to be part of a slothful and highly-politicized organization was seen as professional hara-kiri.

'BCCI is the most abused organization in India. But I could see Modi's vision. Our common vision was to make IPL the best sporting league in the world. It was probably for the first time BCCI was moving towards service orientation from being a monopolist. And it wanted to do it through good governance. I don't think people get an opportunity to work on such projects too often,' reminisced Raman.

The four months leading to the IPL finals were the busiest in Raman's life. BCCI has hundreds of honorary office bearers and administrators for its board, but for a venture that was built from scratch in about 120 days, it chose to have a team of four including Modi, his secretary Radhika, Raman, and the tournament director, Dhiraj Malhotra. The team didn't even have an office of its own, and operated out of a corner of the BCCI's Mumbai HQ and five-star hotel rooms. That the tournament went off without many glitches with only the four-member team handling event management, logistics, thousands of media queries and controversies such as the one about skimpily-clad cheerleaders was a miracle in itself. 'Speed was of greatest importance. With the timelines we were given, I don't think anyone in our team slept for more than four hours a day,' said Raman. In fact, not many expected IPL to happen. 'We were briefing a few investment bankers and sports marketing agencies in New York, and when we told them that a league of this scale and ambition was to be rolled out in three months, they nearly fell off their seats. They thought we were out of our minds,' explained Nayar. It was totally a rush job, but then that's how things happen in India. It looks chaotic, but everything somehow seems to miraculously fall into place at the last possible minute.

A week after IPL started, when it became clear that it was a 'soaring' success, the cockiness of Modi was clear. What he didn't say, and what others admitted, was that the entire IPL business model relied heavily on hefty dosages of luck. It was exactly like that last-ball-finish at the IPL finals, where fortuitous nicks and a missed run out at a crucial stage helped Rajasthan Royals walk away with the glory. Like the finals, the start of IPL could have swung either way, it could have been a huge failure.

IPL's first success was selling of the eight city franchises for $724 million. Since there was little clarity about the financial viability of the model, and because the tenders were invited at a notice of about 48 hours, most business houses had little time to do valuations and due diligence. Back then, the $111.9 million that RIL forked out for Mumbai Indians, or a similar amount that Mallya's UB Group spent on Bangalore Royal Challengers, was considered outrageous by those who lost out at the bidding stage and those who couldn't put in a bid due to paucity of time.

To put it in perspective, in 2006, Randy Lerner, an American businessman who owns the NFL team Cleveland Browns, purchased Aston Villa, the fourth most successful club in English football with a 135-year history, for $115 million – or roughly the same amount that Mukesh spent for Mumbai Indians. Lerner's acquisition brought him a readymade fan base (Aston Villa is the biggest club in English midlands), an established tradition and tangible assets that included nearly $50 million worth of real estate in Birmingham. In comparison, the Indian businessman was simply buying a promise for a great and profitable potential in the future.

Not one to mince words, Kishore Biyani, chairman of the largest publicly-traded retail firm, Future Group said that the bidding proved that logic and business sense had taken a back seat. 'IPL is nothing but a game of egos. I'm glad my company is not part of it,' he then said. Future Group did attempt a bid but was disqualified for not making it in time and lost out in the title sponsorship race to the real estate giant, DLF.

Before the bidding, interest levels were raised when ninety Indian firms and several international consortia picked up the franchise auction offer document, priced close to $10,000 each. Persistent rumours of international celebrities such as Russell Crowe teaming up with Bollywood celebrity SRK, added to the excitement. It certainly helped raise IPL's profile and consequently the overall franchise valuations.

On 24 January 2008, on the day of the reckoning, the Wankhede Stadium that has played host to many memorable Test matches turned into a playground for billionaires keen to indulge in a bit of fantasy cricket. The car park at the Vinoo Mankad Gate was an indication of the big bucks barreling into Indian cricket. There was Preity Zinta and Ness Wadia's black Lexus and Dabur Group's scion Mohit Burman's silver Rolls

Royce. Mallya arrived in a red Bentley, with another red Mercedes waiting, just in case the Bentley broke down.

The two Ambani brothers, Mukesh and Anil, were the odd-makers' favourites to dominate the process. There was near certainty that one of them would surely bag the Mumbai Indians franchise. Given their rancorous business rivalry, a few BCCI officials expected the bids for Mumbai Indians to be nearly three times the floor price. Journalists outside the BCCI HQ speculated about the cricketers that the two brothers had on their wish list, and the possibility of the two star-studded Ambani teams fighting it out for the trophy in the finals.

At around 2 p.m., when the bids were opened, the second floor boardroom at the BCCI HQ had barely enough room to seat the fifty-odd executives representing the bidders.

In the final analysis, it was fortunate that IMG and BCCI got the bids that they received. Their gargantuan effort to hard sell IPL to 1,200 companies and individuals around the world seemed like a wasted one. After all, there were only ten bids fulfilling all the technical and financial criteria for the eight teams that were up for grabs.

The bids from Sahara Group, Future Group and ICICI Ventures, the investment arm of ICICI Bank, came in a few hours after the deadline for submitting the offer documents and were, therefore, rejected. DLF couldn't sit on the table due to a few technical inadequacies in its bid. Representatives of Sahara, Future and ICICI landed up on the day of the teams' bidding and made a desperate plea to be included. 'A senior executive from ICICI Ventures made a 45-minute presentation requesting to be allowed to participate in the bidding process,' said a BCCI official present at the auction. The BCCI wanted to include them as it would reflect well on the Board if there were thirteen suitors, instead of the ten who qualified. Indeed, there was a frantic attempt to accommodate the late comers, but the original ten short-listed finalists shot down this move. Legally, BCCI or Modi couldn't do anything. They had to go with the ten bids.

'We were extremely fortunate to get the valuations that we got. With merely ten eligible bidders for eight properties, there could easily have been a cartelization with companies mutually agreeing to take one team each and bidding not more than the floor price of $50 million. Luck was on our side,' admitted a top BCCI functionary, who was part of the auction process.

Anil Ambani's R-ADAG and a consortium led by Deutsche Bank were the lowest bidders and, therefore, failed to grab any franchise. The uncharacteristically conservative bids from the younger Ambani, whose earlier business deals indicated a no-price-too-high-for-me attitude, took many by surprise. Sources contend that his bids were uniformly lower, in the region of $50-60 million for all the city teams on the block. In most cases, Anil's bid wasn't even the second highest one.

The reason was simple: Anil is possibly the shrewdest financial brain of India Inc. He knows clearly when he should over-bid and if the acquisition target is critical for his group. But he realizes when he can get something cheap – and for a song. He is a smart businessman who analyzes the financial pros and cons to the tenth decimal point. For example, when the then combined Reliance Group was planning to take over the *Observer* publication in the 1990s, Anil told journalists that he wouldn't pay too much for it. In fact, he maintained privately that *Observer* should pay him since it was saddled with losses.

Similarly, in the case of IPL teams, he – like many others – thought that the pay-off time was years away. The teams would make losses for the first three to four years. Hence, he didn't want to pay too much and put in extremely conservative bids.

Deutsche Bank, a surprise entrant whose bids were reportedly in the vicinity of $50 million per team, had no immediate strategic interests in either India (as a market) or in cricket. Moreover, among foreign banks in India, Deutsche's presence in the country is significantly smaller than other international banks such as Citibank or Standard Chartered. The only reason why it took part in IPL bidding was because of Anshu Jain, the bank's head of global markets and one of the most influential financiers in the world. As a passionate cricket fan, the London-based Jain convinced Deutsche's management to join the IPL fray. Jain's interest in cricket – and IPL – didn't wane despite the poor show at the bidding. Jain (in his personal capacity) acquired a 10 per cent stake in Mumbai Indians for $20 million.

Many other Indian and global corporates, which had earlier evinced an interest in IPL backed out at the last minute because of several reasons. Some of the notable absentees included billionaire Sunil Mittal's Bharti Enterprises, Vodafone, the Munjal family that controls India's largest two-wheeler firm Hero Honda, and the venerable Tata Group.

For many of these promoters, owning a city franchise would have come in the way of projecting their firms as pan-Indian. At least Bharti and Vodafone felt this. Mittal's Bharti, for instance, traces its corporate origins to Punjab and is headquartered in Delhi. Even when it began its telecom operations in Mumbai, it had to fight the 'outsider' tag. 'We have assiduously tried over the years to build a pan-Indian brand identity for Airtel. We don't want to be seen as a Delhi or north Indian company. The telecom business is all about the widest possible reach. And for the largest telecom company in India, it would have been counter-productive to be associated with one city,' explained a senior Bharti executive. Vodafone had similar concerns, but it made sure it didn't miss the IPL gravy train totally as it signed up as one of the official sponsors of the tournament.

However, the disappointment with junior Ambani's bids was partially offset as Bollywood's Numero Uno, SRK grabbed the Kolkata franchise, and Preity Zinta got hold of Mohali. Fortunately for IPL and BCCI, the two substantially raised the glamour quotient of the league. It was sure to woo sponsors and help get more out of broadcast rights.

The other surprise at the auction was the entry of a little-known consortium, Emerging Media headed by a London-based entrepreneur Manoj Badale, with co-investors such as Rupert Murdoch's estranged son Lachlan, and Modi's brother-in-law Suresh Chellaram, who owns the Nigerian trading and consumer goods marketing firm, Chellaram Plc. Emerging Media bagged the rights for the Jaipur franchise for $67 million, which was the cheapest price paid by any franchisee.

Soon after the bidding, Modi triumphantly claimed that all the cities had found multiple bidders and even those that missed the bus – such as Cuttack, Ahmedabad, Gwalior and Kanpur – had received bids that were above the BCCI's base prices. The IPL plan was that only the top eight bids for the city teams (out of a list of twelve cities) would be included originally. Two other teams would be added later, one each after every three years. The four cities that got the lowest bids during the bidding process were left out.

However, Modi's comment seemed like a bold boast since all the city teams received some bids or the other only because a bidder could bid for as many teams as it wanted, but retain only one even if it was the highest bidder for the others cities. So, a Mukesh Ambani or a Vijay Mallya could bid – and some of them did – for all the cities.

'In hindsight, the bidders who failed, and those who shied away, were too conservative. Yes, it was an untested format but they probably did not factor in the opportunity premium. After all, the teams would be there for perpetuity. And if you look at the balance sheets of the large companies that were initially interested in making a bid, they are sitting on huge pile of cash, even if you discounted the massive personal wealth of some of the promoters. If they hoped to get in during the second round of franchise expansions, the new properties on offer would be second rate, and the valuations of the older ones several times the $112 million that the Mumbai team went for,' reasoned a senior IMG executive.

This has turned out to be true. Just before the start of the second season, glamour girl Shilpa Shetty and Raj Kundra, paid over $15 million to buy a nearly 12 per cent stake in Rajasthan Royals. This implied that the Jaipur franchise was valued at around $125 million, or nearly twice the $67 million that the original owners paid.

In another development, Hyderabad's Deccan Chargers officially mandated KPMG to seek a buyer for the team. In the past, NRI businessman and promoter of Australian retail chain, Retravision, the principal sponsor of the Western Australia cricket team, was interested in a minority stake. But the talks seem to have been called off.

CRICKET COMMERCIAL

Franchise auction was the first step in making the IPL work, and its success was akin to a first ball six. There was still a long way to go, or rather a lot of cricket to be played before the tournament began. However, the media pronounced IPL a huge commercial success. The standard argument was if Ambani and Mallya, who ran business empires, were putting in their millions, there couldn't be anything wrong with the format, its business model and Modi's vision.

If the Indian media's reportage was a reflection of the country's state of mind, the average Indian seemed drunk on the success of Indian enterprise in the last decade or so. Mallya buying an ailing Scottish Distillery, or the Tatas taking over a British steelmaker and a struggling automobile company represents the 'Great Global Indian Takeover'. By the same token, the second fastest growing economy in the world, and an economic superpower in the making deserved a multi-billion dollar, world class sporting league to rival the best in Europe or US.

'There has never been anything like this in the history of sports. No competition has come from start to where we are today in such a short space of time, or with more financial success,' Wildblood told *Guardian* after the franchise bidding.

Compared to the franchisee tender, in a much solemn affair, IPL sold the broadcast rights for ten years to the Sony-World Sport Group combine for a little over $1 billion. This price was paid despite the fact that IPL set a seemingly steep floor price of $590 million, or $59 million a year. Just a year back, ESPN Star, after a frustrating, decade-long wait to get back the ICC World

Cup rights, offered the ICC $ 1 billion to telecast all ICC events including the quadrennial World Cups and Champions Trophy for eight years between 2007 and 2015. This, when compared to Sony's IPL deal, looked a discount store bargain.

The current four-year deal (2007-2010) for the broadcast rights of EPL, that includes satellite TV (Sky Sports), pay TV (Setanta Sports), highlights package (BBC), and internet and radio rights is worth £2.7 billion. Sony and Singapore based WSG combine's $1 billion IPL deal is a fourth of EPL media rights. But then the EPL is on for nearly eight months in a year, compared to forty-four days of IPL. Not to forget that IPL was an unknown beast then, whereas EPL had been around for fifteen years.

One has to also understand that India is an extraordinarily difficult country for sports channels. In a sports market like this, the sustainability of the channel depends on the rights it has to telecast live India matches. Buying cricket rights is a messy and opaque business, as Zee's Chandra found out in 2005; it led him to create a rebel league of his own, and to be free of BCCI's machinations.

Not only do television networks have to come through the less-than-professional bidding process, they have to contend with the looming shadow of the state-owned Doordarshan (DD). Despite paying record prices, private television networks have been forced by courts to share the feed for all the ODI's involving India, which are deemed as 'events of national importance' by the government, with DD at throwaway prices. (One judgement said that in India where cricket is almost a religion, and passions run high, an India match is indeed a matter of national importance, a time when time itself stops for the nation.)

In addition, there is no financial benchmark for channels to arrive at fair valuations. Whenever the rights come up for a renewal, the going rate seems to be more than several times the previous deal, defying all conventional business logic. In 2006, Mumbai entrepreneur Harish Thawani's Nimbus Communication offered BCCI a staggering $612 million in a five-year deal for all international and domestic cricket matches played in India. A similar arrangement between the BCCI and DD for the previous five-year period was a piffling $55 million.

Each new deal makes the previous one look like small change. One of the charges Modi hurled at the previous BCCI regime was that it undersold cricket. And even if a television network successfully managed to bag rights for one event, the resulting capital crunch made it almost impossible for it to fight for the next one.

In the case of IPL, Sony was a surprise candidate because cricket didn't seem to figure in its strategy after its ICC contract ended with the World Cup in 2007.

After the roller coaster ride of the 2003 World Cup, when India made it to the finals, Sony experienced the flip side of beaming live cricket. With the Indian team failing to progress beyond the group stages in both the 2006 Champions Trophy and the 2007 World Cup, cricket was a tiger it had caught by the tail.

Agreed Rohit Gupta, president Sony Entertainment Television, 'In the past four years (before IPL), television ratings of ODIs tapered off. In 2003, the TRPs (television rating point) were in the range of above ten. They came down to as low as three. It clearly showed that viewers didn't have the eight hours to watch an ODI. It meant that youngsters were moving away from cricket, forget about adding new consumers.'

Plus, the speculation about ownership issues at Sony made a renewed crack at cricket rights too much of a distraction for the network. Rumours at that time were that Sony was negotiating with several firms including NRI businessman BK Modi's Spicecorp, and UTV to sell a third of its stake.

'We were playing high-stakes poker with television rights. Although the floor price was $590 million, our internal assessment suggested that there may not be many takers for it. ESPN Star had spent $1 billion for the ICC rights, which left it with little cash to burn on a new venture; Zee and Ten Sports were unlikely contenders and that basically left us with Sony. We were extremely lucky that Sony didn't call our bluff. If it had even bid at the floor price, it would have won the match, thereby making IPL a significantly smaller league than what it's turned out to be today,' revealed a senior BCCI official.

Quite expectedly, out of half a dozen companies that bought the tender documents, only two – Sony and ESPN – bid. In the end, it effectively became a one-horse race.

A couple of days before the deadline, ESPN Software India's MD, RC Venkateish told *The Economic Times*: 'I think the minimum base price for each match in terms of advertising would be $1 million. If someone doesn't try to put in a crazy amount of money into the league, leading to extremely high valuations for the property, we would seriously like to invest in the domestic cricket property.' He probably didn't expect a higher bid. His network's final offer was below the reserve price, while NDTV which had the financial backing of Providence Capital, a US-based PE firm, backed out at the last minute, making the lone Sony's billion-dollar bid seem crazy indeed.

Sony's association with cricket started in 2002 when it won the rights to ICC events for $200 million and is remembered most for introducing the 'oomph' factor in cricket coverage with starlet Mandira Bedi, dressed in noodle straps and tank tops, anchoring the telecast in place of stuffy male experts. 'Everyone predicted our model to be a disaster. Instead, we turned it into a major success. We fundamentally changed the way cricket was sold by television companies until 2003,' said Sony's Gupta.

Under the IPL deal, Sony would fork out close to $918 million to the league administrators while spending an assured $108 million to promote the tournament over ten years. The payment would be staggered with close to $62 million paid every year for the first five years, and a doubling of that amount for the next five. Pre-tournament estimates predicted Sony would make a $4 million loss in the first year, but as the event gathered steam, it turned the formbook on its head.

'Initially, we struggled to get sponsors. We had six instead of seven or eight that we wished for. It wasn't bad but not a great start either. Pricing the advertising slots to sell even 60-70 per cent of the inventory was a challenge. We set base prices for ten years, and were ready to take a hit for the first four years. Instead, we ended up with a profit of $75 million in the first year. We understood cricket and that's why we bet on it,' gloated Gupta.

It took less than a month before those who claimed Sony's $1 billion IPL deal unsustainable and suicidal, changed their tack to argue that IPL rights were sold for a song. 'IPL rights were sold too low. It will prove disastrous for the franchisees because television money is the biggest revenue generator for them. At any rate, the BCCI made a mistake by signing a ten-year deal. Most football telecast contracts around the world are for five years,' claimed Anirban Das Blah, former CEO, Globosport, a sports marketing firm floated by tennis star Mahesh Bhupathi.

'All long-term media rights for sports would appear undervalued. In the case of IPL it was a risk both parties had to undertake. Don't forget that it involves concept building too, which is Sony's responsibility,' defended IPL's COO Raman.

Sony now claims that since it was not a sports channel – it had the experience of making the game more appealing to new set of viewers such as women (during 2003 World Cup), and understood the needs of the Hindi hinterlands, which were being forced-fed a form of cricket intended for urban markets by other sports channels – it was able to sell IPL the right way.

'We are a mass-based Hindi entertainment platform; we are not ESPN. The bulk of our audience is in rural India and our appeal goes deeper than sports channels. Our pitch was that we could draw in more viewers because we can enable the marriage of cricket with entertainment,' said Gupta. He also added, 'We understand entertainment better. We had done it once, and we were sure we could change viewership patterns once again. This got Modi interested. We made it clear that matches have to be in the 3-3.5 hours format like the NBA or EPL, and all the matches would have to be at a time when the family could watch them. It had to fit in with global trends.'

Sony's assessment was that viewers were taking cricket for granted with ODIs becoming too predictable. The game had to be a television reality show, day after day. 'There had to be some action of some sort all the time. There could never be a dull moment during the entire period of the match. The matches did eventually keep the viewers hooked,' Gupta explained. Incidents such as Harbhajan Singh slapping S Sreesanth, and Shane Warne engaging in a slanging match with Sourav Ganguly only added more spice to the script.

However, during Sony's presentations to advertising agencies and advertisers who spent big on sports, the most frequently asked question was why more cricket when TRPs for even the high-profile matches were plummeting. So, Sony vigorously wooed first-time advertisers such as Max New York Life, which had never been associated with cricket. 'We had to convince them that the chances of success were more because the format itself was powerful and was on prime time. We didn't have the numbers to prove it, so the big-ticket advertisers such as Nokia and Maruti Udyog stayed away. Others like Vodafone believed in the concept. We started by selling ten-second slots for Rs 200,000 and, by the semi-finals and finals, the rates shot up to Rs 10,00,000,' revealed Gupta.

ESPN Star sold the most-watched India-Pakistan T20 World Cup finals at the then record price tag of Rs 7,50,000 per slot. A Mumbai-based stock broking house, Alchemy, using the higher-than-usual T20 World Cup ad rates as the benchmark estimated that Sony could generate revenues of Rs 275 crore in the first year, which could go up to Rs 770 crore in the tenth year, when the deal expired. But Sony hit such estimates for a six and managed sales in excess of a whopping Rs 650 crore in the first season. The income from the forty-four days of IPL matches represented 6.5 per cent of India's Rs 10,000 crore television advertising market.

Sony changed the television viewing patterns, and roped in a new set of cricket fans. Twenty-nine-year-old Shobita is one such example. An avid television watcher, she had never liked cricket but somehow got hooked to the T20 format during the World Cup. 'Like the IPL, I watched the World Cup with equal fervour, and found my favourite players, especially Dhoni. I liked the pace of the format, and also the excitement. I liked the fact that the game could turn this way or the other in minutes – just like life. I liked Dhoni because he maintained his cool in tough situations. I really admire and respect this quality in people. I can't remember any one moment when I got fascinated with T20. It gradually happened over a period. I watched one match, liked it, saw another one, and so on.

'Sometimes, while watching a match I would say "Oh, that's a wide". Or use some similar cricketing jargon. And I would pause for a second and think: "Did I really say that?" I mean, until last year, I couldn't even recognize the members of the Indian cricket team. Once they were showing Sreesanth on television and I asked my father if he was a Sri Lankan player. That was the extent of my knowledge of the game before the T20 World Cup.

'Some of the incidents I remember from IPL include Shah Rukh Khan being there to cheer his boys, Ganguly losing his cool, the expressions on the newcomers' faces when they took the wickets of established players, and the manner in which Dhoni would put his arm around a bowler's shoulders and speak to him.

'In T20, I got to see all kinds of emotions so fast. Each match seems like a fast-paced movie. Given a choice between watching a good flick or an IPL match, I would prefer IPL. It would be topical and everyone in the family can watch it together. In case of a movie, every member would have a different taste. If I was watching television alone, I would flip between the movie and the match.'

When IPL got over, thousands of IPL-crazy viewers like Shobita didn't know what to do in the evenings for weeks. They would miss the matches, crave for them, and got bored with any other programmes on television. It was like a constant, guaranteed source of excitement had vanished from their evenings.

However, as the global meltdown hit India, Sony realized that the second season of IPL may not be as lucrative as the first, even if it could rope in more fans for the matches. The buzz in the advertising circles was that many advertisers would shy away from IPL, or demand heavily discounted rates. One controversy is enough to indicate the financial pressures on Sony. For the second season, Anil Ambani's DTH venture, Big TV, paid Rs 137 crore to become an official on-ground sponsor.

But in order to maximize revenues, Sony signed on Big TV's rival DTH service provider Airtel Digital TV as the flagship television advertiser this year. The younger Ambani was in no mood to put up with what he perceived as Airtel's ambush marketing strategy. He pulled out of the deal leaving IPL poorer by Rs 137 crore.

Modi's men immediately swung into action with their strong-arm tactics. Despite being IPL's biggest financial backer, Sony was forced to eat the humble pie. Its CEO, Kunal Dasgupta was forced to resign, and the company agreed to fork out Rs 137 crore to compensate IPL.

In fact, IPL put further pressure on Sony. Citing bad coverage of the matches in 2008, it started looking for a new broadcaster. Modi was technically right since WSG, and not Sony had the main telecast rights for the IPL matches. A peeved Sony went to the court, which stated that the original rights did indeed rest with WSG. Finally, IPL allowed Sony to telecast the matches, but only after the broadcaster agreed to pay more money to the BCCI in 2009. But it was clear that the economic downturn and the change in venue from India to South Africa were having an impact on IPL. Sponsors, organizers, and owners were desperately trying to boost revenues. Several teams that thought they would make a profit in the second year realized that they would have to wait for at least one more year.

DHONI, DHONI ... GONE

It is surprising that the most-hyped component of IPL's first season – the players' auction – turned out to be its smallest commercial component. With each team allowed a shopping kitty of just $5 million, a possible $40 million worth of transaction paled in comparison with the big bucks IPL raked in by selling franchises and other commercial rights.

But on 20 February 2008, as franchisees, managers, stars and cricketers gathered at Mumbai's Hilton Tower, this thought never occurred to any one as they felt that they were in the thick of an event that was the most eagerly awaited part of IPL. It was the game before the game. It was the grand auction for the best of cricketers. Pitting fantasy teams and thematic XIs (like Bradman's Invincibles or Clive Lloyd's Calypso Kings) against each other is an enduring pastime among sports nuts. However, the cricket's version of Monopoly that one witnessed that day was played by some of the richest and the most popular men and women in India – and was for real.

Most of the owners settled in at around 10.30 a.m. for what would be a long day of bargaining in the world's latest talent bazaar. All the IPL's beautiful people, as is their wont, were there in full regalia. While the franchise sale was a straightforward public opening of tenders, players' auction called for greater on-the-spot strategizing and decision-making. That explained why most of the promoters, with the notable exception of Mukesh Ambani, chose to be personally present throughout the auction. In hindsight, the BCCI could be ruing the decision not to employ a similar process for selling franchises because a head-on, real-time clash of billionaire egos could have resulted in bigger spoils as cricketers and sports lovers were soon to find out.

On offer were seventy-eight cricketers who, in IPL organizers' opinion, were the best cricketers in the world. IPL got the British auctioneer, Richard Madley to handle the proceedings. The team's composition rules were simple. Each franchisee was allowed to own up to eight overseas players, but only field four of them in a match. A minimum of four local players and a similar number of youngsters from the BCCI U-22 pool had to be included in a team. Five out of the eight franchises had to compulsorily include one star player from their city, chosen by BCCI and classified as the 'icon' player.

Ergo, the icon players including Sachin Tendulkar (Mumbai), Yuvraj Singh (Mohali), Virender Sehwag (Delhi), Sourav Ganguly (Kolkata), and Rahul Dravid (Bangalore) would not be part of the auction, and instead had to perforce be part of their respective franchise squads. They would be paid 15 per cent more than the most expensive player that their franchise owner paid for in the auction. All the seventy-eight players were assigned base prices according to what BCCI perceived was their ability and commercial potential.

The auction got off to a dream start as India's ODI and T20 skipper, Dhoni was snapped up for a mind-boggling $1.5 million by India Cements Chennai Super Kings in the very first round of trade within minutes of the whole process kicking off. Even before a single ball was bowled, the Super Kings had become a force to reckon with. According to sources present in the hotel, India Cements' chairman N Srinivasan decided not to wait-and-watch once Dhoni was put on the block. He quickly upped the price to $1.5 million, and didn't allow the stunned rivals in the room much time to think about raising the stakes further.

'Dhoni is a four-in-one package. He is one of the best batsmen, a great wicketkeeper, a very astute captain and one of the most loved cricketers in India. We wanted him at any cost,' said Srinivasan. In the same round, he also bagged the world's highest wicket-taker, Muttiah Muralidaran for $600,000. As a Sri Lankan cricketer of Tamil origin, he was an obvious choice for the Chennai team. In the absence of a homegrown icon player, Muralidaran, a source of Tamil pride either side of the Palk Strait (and married to a Chennai girl), was in effect the team's 'local' face.

Hyderabad's Deccan Chargers played a big hand in the opening round, as it bid $700,000 for the destructive, but just retired, Adam Gilchrist. VVS Laxman was nominated as the franchise's icon player, but Laxman voluntarily gave up the status to free up the city's owner's coffers to buy better players at the auction. His magnanimity – since he could be purchased at a lower price now – helped the Deccan Chargers to acquire the services of the other four-in-one player, Andrew Symonds, for $1.35 million. Symonds became the most expensive overseas player purchased, and only the second millionaire cricketer in IPL.

Although Mumbai's icon player, Tendulkar was away in Australia playing the tri series, the franchise managers appeared to have carried out his player selection. His two best friends, Sanath Jayasuriya and Harbhajan Singh (barely a month ago, Tendulkar's strong testimony saved Bhajji's career in the racial abuse case against Symonds) were in the Ambani camp for $975,000 and $850,000, respectively.

The Emerging Media-owned Rajasthan Royals' strategy was to mop up players such as Graeme Smith, Kamran Akmal and Younis Khan at their floor price without getting involved in the fierce bidding game. In fact, the franchisee did not purchase a single overseas player above his floor price. Its two of the most expensive signings were Mohammad Kaif ($650,000) and Yusuf Pathan ($475,000). Manoj Badale's 'Uncle Scrooge' strategy attracted a financial penalty from the IPL management for failing to spend the stipulated minimum $3.3 million at the auction.

For those who were not privy to the players' auction, it turned out to be a mix of theatrics, dramatics, tensions, anxiety, relief, laughter, sorrow and extreme boredom. There were moments that depicted everything from glamour to sports. The teams' tables itself offered a fascinating sight. There were teams such as Kolkata, Bangalore and Mohali that crowded their specific round tables with at least a dozen people. Kolkata had SRK and Ganguly, among others with open laptops. Preity Zinta and Ness Wadia were seen talking, laughing, whispering, and cheering at the Mohali table. And one could see Mallya and Dravid having several whispered conversations throughout the auction.

Jaipur offered the saddest sight. Its table seemed to be tucked away in a darkish corner. In fact, it seemed to be in the shadow of all the other tables, which were bright and energetic. Only four people sat on the Jaipur table, unlike thrice that number on others. A couple of open laptops were the only indication that the quartet owned an IPL team and had come to bid for star players. During most of the auction time, they sat and watched silently as other teams aggressively bid for famous cricketers. Only on a few occasions did one see the enthusiasm among the four people who represented the Jaipur team.

There were some very memorable moments too during the auction. For instance, when the bids started for Laxman, everyone was keen to see if Hyderabad can get him. The bidding war was between Hyderabad and Kolkata. Eventually, when the Deccan Chargers got him, there were loud claps and huge cheers.

In the case of intense bidding, as was the case with potentially great T20 players such as Jayasuriya and Symonds, the atmosphere was charged. Several teams like Chennai, Bangalore, Hyderabad and Mumbai put in bids at regular intervals for the Sri Lankan opener. During the last stages, there were nervous laughs from the Hyderabad table. Finally, Mumbai got him.

In the case of Symonds, it was Hyderabad versus Bangalore versus Mumbai. The Hyderabad contingent kept tapping their fingers unsure whether it will get this hard hitter from Down Under. Mumbai also tried its best. Finally, when Hyderabad won this player, its contingent members – as did others – clapped, laughed, cheered and heaved sighs of relief.

Preity Zinta of Kings XI Punjab was one of the feistiest promoters in the room. She hugged her co-promoter Ness when Mohali got Australian fast bowler Brett Lee. Excited during the bidding for Indian fast bowler Zaheer Khan, she kept laughing nervously – and constantly, as Ness took a few sips of water while waiting for the process to be over. Both jumped from their seats when Mohali finally bagged Khan.

Laissez-fair it may have been, but some of the player purchases defied cricketing and business logic. It took some players a while to get used to the idea of being bought and sold. Gilchrist was the first to voice his discomfort. 'There was a little element of feeling like a cow. But it's interesting and unique. There is a slight uneasiness. But let us allow it to settle down,' he said after the auction.

The Australian media was shocked to find that there were not many takers for their captain and one of the world's best batsmen, Ricky Ponting. The Tasmanian run-machine was sold to Kolkata Knight Riders for a paltry $400,000, a meagre improvement of $65,000 over his floor price, whereas some of the

Indian youngsters like Manoj Tiwari, who was yet to make a run in international cricket, commanded $675,000.

'I thought I might have been able to attract a little bit more than that,' quipped Ponting after learning about his second-class citizenship in IPL. Mike Hussey, the man they call 'Mr Cricket' back in Australia, and Glen McGrath, the ace pacer, remained unsold in the first round. Hussey's uncapped younger brother David, nicknamed Bomber, who plays for Victoria was shocked when he was told that he had commanded a $625,000 price tag. 'He (Mike) actually sent me a text message that morning and said, "I can't believe you're worth double of what I am," said an embarrassed David Hussey.

'I just don't understand someone like Brad Hodge valued less than me. He is one of the best T20 players in the world, no question about it. His record for Lancashire and Victoria is second to none. It doesn't make any sense at all.'

Not all Indian players were thrilled with their newfound net worth. Indian Test opener Wasim Jaffer was bought by the Bangalore Royal Challengers for $100,000 – the lowest for an Indian player. Neither he nor his wife could figure out why. 'After the auction, my wife phoned to tell me who got what. She was very upset and sad that other players had got more. Obviously it hurts. I have proved myself, and I have made runs in Test cricket, over 2,000 of them,' said a crestfallen Jaffer in an interview.

'The auction was a simple case of free market economics taking over. There was a limited pool of players' talent available from which to choose. And the franchise owners reacted to the basic law of demand and supply. Players that the franchise owners felt would boost their teams and draw in the crowds were in more demand,' felt Modi.

DIVIDED LOYALTIES

Maybe Modi was right. But another debate that was sparked off by IPL was about the reasons why successful businessmen and film stars buy city teams. Refining crude oil or constructing an airport or a steel plant is one thing, and owning a star-studded cricket franchise in a country where the game enjoys the status of religion, quite another. If it was all about creating wealth and generating better returns, surely there are different opportunities in India's fast-growing economy.

Do these corporate billionaires have a feel for the game, or understand the dejection and elation that fans go through whenever their team lost or won? For puritans, the IPL meant an end of cricket's age of innocence. Cricket is perhaps one of the few team sports with reasonable fan following, where players make their reputations as well as earn big bucks only if they manage to play for the national teams. Aspirants of various age groups, who play for their clubs, districts, states, or zones – in any of the mainstream cricket-playing country – think only of how to get into the national team.

In a single stroke, IPL changed this mindset – forever. Today, each player, whether he's playing U-19, U-22, or Ranji Trophy, is a mercenary of sorts. He is probably thinking of getting into an IPL team, and only play for the franchise owners or wealthy benefactors in a bid to make them happy and richer.

'The exploitation of the game in IPL is too naked. Patriotism which has sustained the game for more than a century is replaced by narcissism,' felt Santosh Desai, CEO, Future Brands and a veteran of the advertising industry.

'Look at it from another angle. IPL has monetized cricket in many ways. Where'll most of the money that BCCI makes from IPL go? Right back into domestic cricket. Businessmen are in IPL because they see good business in it. It's a consumer business platform like no other,' defended IPL COO Raman.

BCCI bigwigs also scoff at the criticism that IPL is a sellout of cricket at the altar of Mammon. They are quick to point out that the criticism sticks better on ICL, the rebel cricket league, which by its very design furthers the business interests of Subhash Chandra and Essel Group.

But one has to accept the fact that IPL was created on the basis of what audiences want to watch on television, and the current rage seems to favour reality shows. 'With IPL, cricket is taking a fresh guard. There is a sea change underway in the consumer space and we are merely recalibrating the cricket package to suit changing preferences. The consumer today wants instant gratification and better entertainment with no predictability,' explained Raman. It also helped that India discovered T20 by accident and in a manner resembling an unscripted reality show.

When India won the inaugural T20 World Cup in Johannesburg, the romantic narrative was that a young, ragtag team cobbled together at the eleventh hour due to the injuries and withdrawal of established stars, went out and captured the world. And with a style and swagger that had never been seen before in Indian teams.

'IPL has little cricketing logic, but sound television logic. The Indian youth wants to watch big names and celebrity parties, where the camera has an obsessive focus on the cleavage. They want a Bollywood awards show with a dash of instant-result cricket,' argued Desai.

Sony kick-started the process of expanding the game's appeal with Mandira Bedi hosting the 2003 World Cup coverage; IPL flattened it further to make cricket into little bite-sized exotic sushi rolls in attractive bento boxes with a generous helping of wasabi. The idea of expanding the market is a bit like converting a cloistered clubhouse into a quick-service family restaurant that offers something for everybody.

'Cricket was desperately in need of fresh ideas because at least in the big metros it was losing kids to EPL. Children had begun to think of cricket as the dad's game,' said Harsha Bhogle, and pointed to his son wearing an Arsenal football club jersey.

'Cricketers must perform to fans' satisfaction; they must account for every paisa spent on them (already newspapers have created a 'Paisa Vasool Index' to figure out how much every run has cost) or else they can get publicly upbraided. What IPL has done is to take cricket and pack in the best names, compress it in a timeframe that makes it easy to consume and sell it to viewers, broadcasters and advertisers alike,' explained Desai.

In a bid to encourage viewers, team owners and experts do

this constant evaluation of price versus performance of the IPL players. *The Times of India* created its own Value Index. In one of the articles, the writer said: 'We assigned batting, bowling and fielding points to each player based on his performance. We also assigned captaincy points based on team performance. We then totaled up all these points.

'The batting points were worked out on the principle that T20 is not only about how much you score, but how fast you get the runs. We, therefore, worked out the average strike rate for all batsmen in IPL so far, which turned out to be very nearly 130. The number of batting points each player got was the runs scored by him multiplied by his strike rate and divided by the average strike rate of 130.'

However, instant gratification, a euphemism for consumer fickleness, which fuelled IPL's success in the inaugural season, can be a double-edged sword. It forces television channels to run crassly-titled post-match analysis shows such as 'Match ke Mujrim' or 'Villains of the Match'. In time, the viewers can get bored and reach out for the remote. Even KBC, IPL's paradigm-changing predecessor, was dead in three seasons.

Just think about this: How many last-ball finishes, sixers and hat-tricks can one absorb in a span of forty-four days? One of IPL's biggest challenges in the future will be to avoid jading of the appetite for instant cricket. There could be supply-side problems as well. In a slowing economy, the promoters' willingness to plough in money into a newborn league could be severely tested, and the astronomical rates at which Sony had sold advertising slots in the first year could become unsustainable.

IPL's long-term commercial success and its ability to withstand business cycles is directly linked to sustaining public interest in the league. In a format where cricket is the normal pull factor, patriotism is irrelevant; the eyeballs would depend on the quality and intensity of all the matches in a season. The $5 million player salary-cap in the first season of IPL was meant to achieve a certain parity between all the eight teams to maintain a balance and ensure that all the matches were interesting.

But, this can change if IPL rules allow players to be bought and sold for any amount, thereby making it difficult for teams with lesser means to be competitive. And 'David' Rajasthan Royals might never be able to beat Goliath Chennai Super Kings again.

Such criticisms are now becoming common about other professional and privatized sports events like EPL and NBA. In the case of EPL, the Abu Dhabi United Group, which is the private equity arm of the UAE's ruling family, recently created a stir by buying out Manchester City. Arsene Wenger, Arsenal football club's cerebral manager who has a master's degree in economics, wondered about the oil sheiks' sudden interest in English football. 'It doesn't look like they are there to make any money. So ... then why are they buying it, is it out of love? Well, I am not sure these people are supporters of Manchester City from a young age. Why are they doing it?,' he told the club's official magazine.

The craze for asset ownership had characterized the Indian market over the last five years. If it was real estate, cars and stocks for the middle-class Indians, their richer compatriots wanted assets at a much grander scale. So, they built twenty-seven-storey residences, bestowed personal jets on spouses and made big-ticket overseas acquisitions. They were on a constant lookout for new asset classes that would reflect their lifestyles, and put them on par with the global aristocracy of the rich.

According to the 2008 *Forbes* list of richest people, four of the top eight billionaires in the world are Indians. Moreover, with thirty-six billionaires compared to Japan's twenty-four, India is the moneybags capital of Asia. A Merrill Lynch and Cap Gemini report estimated that India's population of millionaires grew 20 per cent in 2007 to about 100,000. The rate of growth in India was more than twice the growth of millionaires in the US.

For billionaires in the developing world like India, owning a sports team became a fashionable accouterment to flaunt. What better way to do it than buying the forbidden fruit called Indian cricket, which, for far too long, had been the preserve of politicians and their middlemen. Already, there are rumours that

Anil Ambani, who is still smarting from his failure to jump into the IPL gravy train, wants to go one up on his brother by owning an EPL team. His firm R-ADAG denied any interest in the club Newcastle United, but the buzz in the English press refuses to die. Some speculate that he has now trained his sight on Everton football club.

DIVIDING THE PIE

Whether it is football, baseball or cricket, commercialization implies the same thing. In fact, all the major sports leagues in the world operate on a simple and straightforward financial model. It's no different with IPL. There are four major revenue streams for the teams. For smaller clubs in a league, and indeed all the teams in a new format such as the IPL, central revenues distributed by the league's apex body is the largest slice of the cake. IPL's governing body equally distributes 80 per cent of the money earned from selling broadcast rights to all eight teams for the first two years. Subsequently, the figure will reduce to 70 per cent for the next three years, and 60 per cent for the remaining five years of the decade-long deal.

In addition, a flat 60 per cent of central sponsorship, which includes money from title sponsor DLF and others such as Hero Honda, Vodafone and Pepsi, is doled out for ten years to all the teams. This translates into an assured income of $8 million right from year one. The teams get to keep what they earn through ticket sales for matches held in their cities, the sponsorship deals they click independent of the governing body, and sales of merchandises such as replica shirts and assorted souvenirs.

Before the start of IPL, it appeared that the BCCI had sold an unproven asset and a potential lemon to the canniest of businessmen for the price of a limousine, but the $8 million from the central revenue pool virtually cancelled out the sums that owners paid to own their respective teams.

For instance, the $76 million that SRK's firm Red Chillies Entertainment paid for Kolkata Knight Riders has to be paid to IPL over ten years in annual instalments of $7.6 million. Taking into account player salaries, and administrative and promotional expenditure, it is unlikely that Kolkata could incur losses of more than $2-3 million, given the assured revenues of $8 million a year from the IPL pool, even if it doesn't earn any income from other sources.

That's why billionaire businessmen such as Anil Ambani and Kishore Biyani, who lost out in the teams' auction by a few million dollars would be kicking themselves, especially after the initial success of IPL. Now, $2-3 million is just about two weeks' sales at a single Mumbai Big Bazaar store owned by Biyani.

Arsenal, which is one of the EPL's richest clubs, had a turnover of £223 million in 2007-08 with a pre-tax profit of £36.7 million. While EPL's new 2007 television rights deal contributed £68 million to Arsenal's topline, the £95 million from ticket sales was the club's highest source of income. Each time Arsenal played at the 60,000-capacity Emirates stadium in 2007-08, $3 million got added to its revenues. The reason: Arsenal home games were invariably sold out last season; most of the bigger clubs sell season tickets and, at last count, 40,000 people were on Arsenal's waiting list.

As the IPL progresses, the marketing skills of the franchisees in getting bigger sponsorships, forcing more ticket sales and their ability to sell merchandise would differentiate the profitable teams from the losing ones.

While most franchise owners expected to make a profit in the fourth or the fifth year, the rousing start to the IPL has made them optimistic enough to feel that they could be in the black by the end of the second season. However, the current slowdown will upset such expectations. The previous benchmark for a similarly packaged product was the Afro-Asian games that pitched some of the best cricketers from Asia against what was essentially a South African XI. The concept was a complete disaster. Therefore, no one in the BCCI had foreseen success of this magnitude for IPL.

'Even by the most liberal estimates, we expected things to settle down a bit by the third year with teams making a little bit of money by the fifth,' said BCCI's Ratnakar Shetty.

'Profitability and sustainability beyond the forty-four days is an issue to which we don't have too many answers right now,' felt Neil Maxwell, the Australian CEO of the Kings XI Punjab. That's why Modi peddled the idea of having two IPL seasons in a year, instead of one. The existing ICC Future Tours Programme (FTP), the world's cricket calendar drawn up to 2012, doesn't leave too much time for two IPLs in a year.

However, the declining popularity of the 50-overs game and accompanying business considerations could force ICC to accept Modi's proposal. 'We don't want to push things too soon because everybody thinks of BCCI as the big bully of international cricket. Two IPLs in a year is an eventuality. The players themselves would push for it. Just wait and watch,' explained a high-ranking BCCI official.

In April 2008, just a few days before IPL began, the *Sydney Morning Herald* reported the startling results of a players' survey conducted in Australia. Nearly half of the players on a central contract with Cricket Australia, and the six state associations said that they were willing to give up international cricket for playing in IPL, or its rival ICL. And 93 per cent of the players said that they wished to continue playing cricket after retirement, which was a sure shot signal that they would opt for IPL, ICL, or any other similar league that may be launched in the near future. Getting paid between $500,000 and $1 million for playing two months of T20 cricket is quite a steal for retired cricketers.

Already, India has become a fertile land of opportunities for leading past and present Australian cricketers. A few years ago, leading Australian captain Steve Waugh led the way by bagging lucrative sponsorship deals from tyre maker MRF and another Chennai-based insurance firm, AMP Sanmar. Now, Brett Lee, who has appeared in several television commercials in India for brands such as Timex, New Balance shoes, and TVS, is trying hard to expand his Hindi vocabulary beyond *shukriya*.

Lee has made influential friends in India. Preity Zinta and Ness Wadia are close to him (which explains why he turns out for Kings XI), so is Kumar Mangalam Birla, chairman of the $25-

billion AV Birla group. Birla, close enough to exchange text messages frequently with Lee, ensured that the latter was profiled in the *Economic Times*, the country's largest business daily, when Birla was the paper's 'guest' editor for a day on 6 April 2008. Michael Clarke signed up with celebrity management firm Percept Talent Management in 2007 to scour the lucrative endorsement market while former internationals such as Adam Gilchrist and Tom Moody spent a lot of off-the-field time in India padding up for various Australian state trade delegations and universities.

CRICKET AS ENTERTAINMENT

Even as cricketers saw the golden rainbow in IPL, so did the entertainers. The latter realized that IPL had to become like an extended Bollywood film, with cricket thrown in as a mere prop, to grab eyeballs. All the teams queued up to sign brand ambassadors; they also quickly made music videos and created glitzy ads to promote their teams.

SRK was the fastest off the block. His franchise had the biggest stadium in the country at its disposal, and the most fanatical cricket-watching Bengalis to fill it up. 'Even if he does a 10-minute performance of the kind he put up with Saif Ali Khan at the recent Filmfare awards, believe me, the Eden Gardens will be jam packed. Knight Riders is the team to watch out for,' said Fraser Castellino, the former CEO of Rajasthan Royals.

The consensus was that only two teams had a chance to book profits in the first year – and for two completely different reasons. If crowd puller SRK could fill up half the 100,000-seats at Eden Gardens, he could meet his business targets. And he had the money and the talent to bombard Indian living rooms with the right messages.

Advertisers who use SRK to endorse their products can't stop gushing about his star power and the exceptional return on investments his presence guarantees. Ergo, some of them teamed up with him to sponsor the Knight Riders. Nokia, Tag

Heuer and Belmonte, were the first to open their purse strings. The men in black and gold may not have started their IPL campaign well in the first season, but they were commercially the most profitable team with sponsorship deals worth nearly $10 million in the first year. As it turned out, SRK became the biggest attraction in IPL – even bigger than cricketers.

A survey by the *Economic Times* in the eight IPL club cities showed that more viewers watched the matches to see SRK and Preity, rather than the game's legends such as Tendulkar and Ganguly. When asked to recall ten individuals associated with IPL, only five cricketers made it to the list.

In the same survey, the Kolkata team turned out to be the most popular IPL team. It was the first choice team for nearly a third of cricket followers, and even the fans in the big metros, which had strong corporate-backed teams of their own, seemed to be cheering for the Kolkata side. While only a fifth of the Mumbaikars supported Mumbai Indians, 30 per cent were rooting for SRK. In Delhi, nearly a third of the supporters were rooting for Kolkata, and only one in five regarded Delhi Daredevils as their favourite.

The other team that was expected to finish the first year in good financial health was Rajasthan Royals. With the lowest cost overheads it was the cheapest franchise at $67 million and had spent the least ($3.3 million) on players. If Kolkata's mantra was revenue maximization, Jaipur believed in cost optimization. 'Except for a couple of franchises, I don't see too many being bottomline-focused. Looking at some of the players they signed, or their top management, you wonder what they are up to. It's almost scary,' said Globosport's Anirban Blah.

Although he won't name them, Anirban predicted at least three franchise owners would change hands when the BCCI finally expanded the IPL in a few years' time because of bankruptcy or attractive valuations that would allow disinterested team promoters to exit without too many scars. This has already happened with the entry of new investors in Mumbai Indians and Rajasthan Royals.

Jaipur's promoter, Emerging Media, whose investors include Lachlan is an international media rights firm focused on the Indian subcontinent and other cricket-playing regions. It is the only franchise owner whose bread and butter business is cricket. Since 2004, the company, formerly known as Investors in Cricket, focused on building and investing in sports rights. It acquired the commercial rights to Leicestershire County Cricket Club in 2004, staged the first Champions T20 tournament in 2006, and launched a reality television talent hunt for cricketers in India called Cricket Star.

Badale, the London-based chairman of Emerging Media doesn't like the suggestion that Rajasthan Royals owed its success to frugality. 'Our mantra was not cost optimization but to focus on cricketing performance. We spent less on players, simply because we did not buy many players in the first auction. The rules clearly stated that there might be multiple auctions, and we did not believe that the first seventy-eight players were the best T20 players in the world. As other teams ran out of money, we were able to buy players in the later auction. But the strategy was an outcome, not the driver of our business model.'

The Jaipur team spent less on entertainment, Bollywood, and cheerleaders. 'We were the only franchisee which didn't have Bollywood stars dancing at the inaugural event. We tried to display business sense, rather than emotions,' said Castellino. He contended that instead of coughing up Rs 7-10 crore for celebrity signings, he'd rather give out tickets for free to the locals. 'Will Akshay Kumar bring 30,000 people into my ground,' was his retort.

The team's brand ambassador was not a film star, but the Rajasthan state's former chief minister, Vasundhara Raje. In a coup, she turned out for the matches at Jaipur's Sawai Mansingh Stadium wearing designer sarees in the team's royal blue and mustard colours. 'Our belief was always that entertainment was on the pitch,' felt Badale.

Even the company's decision to bid for the Jaipur franchise was not rooted in regional sentiments that some of the other owners were led by. 'We believed Rajasthan Royals would be one of the most profitable franchises, as the majority of the revenues that accrue to franchises come from the central television rights and sponsorship rights, which are divided equally. Yet, we were hopeful that our cost structure would be lower because Jaipur had no 'icon' player, who had to be paid a huge amount. And Jaipur had an extraordinary stadium that had been spruced up only a year back,' explained Badale.

Most of these arguments seem to be retrospective (see Ch. *Skips, Slips and Sighs*). Badale's strategies sound workable and strong, but his connections between cricket and business, between spending money and winning, seem far-fetched. Jaipur was simply lucky to get the players it got, it was unlucky (which turned fortunate) that it could not buy the cricketers it wanted to even at exorbitant prices. Overall, its tactics were simply not as thought through as it is made out now.

However, with the team's IPL win, Badale is confident that the victory will create massive opportunities for the franchise. 'We want to build an international community and Rajasthan/ Gujarat have huge overseas populations. We are thinking of a rollout of a big membership, licensing and merchandising programme, as well as a series of tours to develop the brand internationally.'

Among the eight franchises, Rajasthan Royals, where a clutch of investors rather than a large corporate house own the team, may not have a long-term interest in owning the franchise. Like other PE investors, the owners would cash out if the takeover offer was attractive. It happened to an extent when Shilpa Shetty purchased a minority stake.

'As with any successful business, we are being approached daily with multiple ideas for raising capital to fund future growth. At this stage, we are simply listening to these ideas. Our investors want a return, but unlike a PE house it is "our money", and we are not subject to any exit guidelines or targeted rates of return.'

There could be more deals in the pipeline – like in the case of Deccan Chargers – after the second season. The only hitch could be the current slowdown which may prevent investors from putting in too much money and dissuade IPL promoters as valuations would crash automatically.

Financial sources contend that at the moment the highest valuation is $200 million for Mumbai Indians. So, if a promoter can sell a 20 per cent stake, he can easily recover $40 million, or a major chunk of the money it paid to buy the team.

CRICKET AS BUSINESS

While Badale & Co. are in the business of sports, there were compelling reasons for other businessmen to get into sports. Delhi Daredevils' affable CEO, Yogesh Shetty claims that the combination of sports and business is an unbeatable value creator. 'Any association with world-class sports, let alone owning one of them, has a tremendous positive rub-off effect for the company and the brands it owns,' he explained.

The London-based Shetty knows a bit about the marriage of business and sport. In his previous avatar as the CEO of Travelex' worldwide commercial foreign exchange business, he was instrumental in sponsoring the touring Australian ODI cricket teams, and several other (rugby and football) associations around the world.

Just a week after the IPL season one ended, Shetty was in a hurry to close the financial books, and return to his family in London. Delhi's owner GMR Sports' tiny fourth-floor office in one of the newly refurbished glass- and-chrome buildings in Delhi's Connaught Place could barely accommodate Shetty's twenty-odd colleagues. Recently dismantled vinyl signages and cardboard likenesses of some of the team's stars crowded whatever space there was in the room. A day before the profit-and-loss accounts had to be sent to the auditors, Shetty was fretting over what he thought was an unreasonably high number of free tickets and hospitality coupons doled out during the IPL. His estimates and the actual number of coupons didn't tally.

There's also the problem of outstanding receipts of around Rs 10,00,000 from various agencies. If his accountant wasn't able to chase the creditors, he threatened to call them up himself. But over the maddening two months, the Daredevils' CEO had learnt to work with a smile plastered on his face. After heading a multi-billion dollar MNC, monitoring IPL-like micro issues was a new experience for Shetty. 'The second season would be easier. In two months, you cannot build a new business. For any successful franchise model, there has to be adequate pre-season build up, enough sustained excitement in the post-season. In the first year, all franchises had tactics and no business strategy. It takes a while for businesses to understand the aesthetics of sport.'

GMR Group always wanted to have a presence in sports, IPL or no IPL. The Rs 2,700-crore group had been hard-selling the idea of a corporate-owned cricket league for the past five years to the BCCI. Simultaneously, it was working on proposals to invest in other sports such as tennis, football and hockey.

'IPL took off and cricket fitted into our strategy. The day we won the Delhi franchise, there had to be a structure in place. It's not a lifestyle investment, or something GMR wanted to do only for visibility,' said Shetty. It formed a wholly-owned subsidiary, GMR Sports, and announced that it wished to run it like any other businesses, with a focus on bottomlines and wealth creation.

Not surprisingly, Shetty's conversations were replete with jargons such as brand equity, customer throughput and quality of delivery. In true corporate style, the franchisee even had an induction programme for all its team members, just as it does for its employees. Cricketers were put through sessions on GMR's corporate philosophy and vision, and cultural orientation. The Chennai-based spiritual guru, Swami Sukhabodhananda spoke to players about mind relaxation techniques, and the benefits of enjoying the moment.

'For us, the cricketers were like other employees. There had to be an emotional connect between the team members, and between the team and the employer to be successful. Living away from home for an additional six weeks, apart from their national tours, can be difficult for players who spend nearly 200 days in a year on the road. With players from so many different countries and cultures, the team needed a unique character. We told them that we want the Delhi Daredevils to be the best-loved franchise in the world. During the induction, we reassured players that GMR's mantra was "not what we do, but how we do things". We spoke about how we could make IPL's days fun and joy, not just for the fans but also for ourselves,' explained Shetty.

Even when the team's performances dipped in the final stretch of the league matches in the first season with three consecutive defeats, and when the team's hopes of reaching the semi-finals seemed bleak, members of the promoter family and GMR's top-management met the team over lunch and reassured them of the management trust and commitment.

Shetty expects the Delhi franchise to break even at the end of the second season and believes that the business opportunities would be limitless. 'No one knows the kind of positive spin-offs that IPL will have in the coming years. The risk-based approach of the T20 format means that every moment in the match is a key one. T20 will appeal to new markets such as the US. We haven't even begun to scratch the surface yet,' felt Shetty.

As a lifelong supporter of the east London football club, West Ham United, Shetty thinks that the Delhi Daredevils can become a talent nursery for Indian cricket, just as West Ham is known as the 'Academy of Football' and has nurtured some of the best-known English footballers such as Rio Ferdinand, Joe Cole, and Frank Lampard.

Of all the eight IPL franchise owners, the Chennai-based cement manufacturer, India Cements was among the least-known. It's not the most glamorous of businesses to be in at the best of times, and it doesn't help if you are perceived to be a conservative, publicity-shy, and provincial operator. To most followers of the game, it came as a surprise that the little-known India Cements made the most expensive player purchase in the first season, paying $1.5 million for Dhoni.

Not many knew that cricket is an inseparable part of India Cements. The company's involvement with the game goes back to four decades, and it manages more than a dozen teams, which participate in various divisions of Chennai's city league. It has more than fifty cricketers on its rolls, and leading Indian stars such as Dravid turn out for one of its teams. Several Tamil Nadu cricketers in the Chennai Super Kings team, including S Badrinath, L Balaji and P Amarnath are employees of India Cements. The company's chairman is the president of the TNCA and a key member of Sharad Pawar's cricket cabinet. TNCA almost functions like an India Cements subsidiary. In September 2008, Srinivasan was appointed the BCCI's secretary.

'Right from the time of his bid for the Chennai franchise, Srinivasan had the P&L worked out in his head. I don't think any of the franchise owners knew about the business of cricket better than him,' said an IMG executive.

'It's not as if we were spending (the bid price of) $91 million in one stroke. It's a commitment over ten years. When the media rights got sold for $1 billion, I knew that this alone would cover our franchise acquisition cost,' explained Srinivasan with his eyes closed, and almost half scowling at the naïveté of the query.

The company claimed that Chennai Super Kings was cash positive after the first season. 'The valuation of each property associated with the Super Kings is zooming, which would bring new revenue streams in the future, while our costs at least for the next three years remain fixed,' he revealed. And whether his cricket franchise makes money as a standalone business is the least of his concerns.

As per internal estimates, and the numbers crunched by brokerage firms such as Alchemy, the value of Super Kings is in excess of Rs 600 crore (the figure could be higher now). 'Even if the company spent Rs 1,500 crore on brand promotion for the team, it wouldn't have got a fraction of the publicity that Super Kings got us. The team's brand equity will help us expand our businesses in north India. We have big plans to be a pan-India corporate group,' averred Srinivasan.

'For instance, the cement retailers and distributors in Rajasthan hadn't heard of India Cements. Super Kings would become our calling card. Everyone knows which team Dhoni plays for,' added Rakesh Singh, the head of marketing for both India Cements and its IPL team. Piggybacking on the team's popularity, the company hopes to launch an all-India cement brand, Super Kings, packaged in the team's yellow colour.

Even before the players' auctions, Srinivasan's brief to VB Chandrashekhar, the former Tamil Nadu opener, who manages the cricketing affairs including the selection of the team, was that Super Kings had to be fearless entertainers. The team's brand identity was modelled on a curious mix of personality traits of Boris Becker, Pelé, Bruce Lee, Magic Johnson, and Sylvester Stallone.

At the first 2008 players' auction, most of Srinivasan and Chandrashekhar's picks were heavy hitters. With Dhoni, Mathew Hayden, Jacob Oram, Mike Hussey and Albie Morkel, Super Kings was definitely IPL's muscle-heavy Rambo team. 'Our experience of running teams helped us understand how to manage stars. Several of our local teams are often a mix of iconic stars and little-known youngsters, who aspire to come up through club cricket. Not many IPL teams knew how to do that. Knowing how to handle stars was a big reason for our success,' felt Srinivasan.

But as a franchise that represented a city with a strong sub-culture that was different from the rest of the country, the Super Kings had little geographic identity – be it the team's unimaginative moniker (unsanctioned ICL's Chennai team is called Super Stars), or the brand communication and advertising. Although Chennai's showbiz rivals Bollywood, India Cements leveraged it only to the extent to bring in Tamil Nadu's hottest current star, Vijay as a brand ambassador, who besides making a token appearance or two at press conferences, and matches at the Chepauk Stadium, was mostly ineffectual.

Then there was K Srikkanth, the evergreen former India captain and the best-known Chennai cricketer, fronting for the team from television studios. Incidentally, his son Aniruddha Srikkanth was part of the Chennai squad, but made a solitary appearance without success. There were hardly more than a few local players, like S Badrinath, and S Vidyut Sivaramakrishnan, who could find a place in the starting XI. But that didn't deter the Chennai fans from rooting for their band of mercenaries.

Flashy businessman Mallya, whose personal PR humbles that of either Sir Richard Branson or Donald Trump, never hid the fact that for him Bangalore Royal Challengers was a platform to promote his airlines and liquor brands, which he couldn't advertise through conventional media because of government restrictions.

But since the city-based team's raison d'être is to act as a surrogate advertisement, rather than to emotionally appeal to the fans, the strategy was a flawed one. Therefore, it didn't come as a surprise that the Bangalore franchise was the most troubled of all the eight teams. To be fair, it has to be said that if a discerning and enlightened fan had to pick a favourite IPL team, Bangalore Royal Challengers would have ranked high on the list.

Dravid and Anil Kumble have won more Tests for India with their individual performances than most other players. South Africans, Jacques Kallis and Mark Boucher, and West Indies' Shivnaraine Chanderpaul could walk in to any fantasy XIs. Zaheer Khan was at his peak in 2007, and one of Wisden's five players of the year. South African fast bowling sensation, Dale Steyn had tormented many top batsmen and was named the ICC Test bowler of the year in 2008. If the rest of the IPL teams comprised rocks stars and billboard toppers, Mallya's team had classical maestros.

In what would go down in the history of sports marketing as one of the most insensitive decision, Mallya named the team of gold pedigree after a distinctly middle-of-the-road bottle of Indian Made Foreign Liquor, Royal Challenge. However, when owning a sports team becomes the equivalent of flaunting a fancy pet, there are no holy cows.

The idea that IPL could expand the boundaries of cricket business, and bring in a whole set of consumers to watch the game and, hence, buy their products, is a seductive one. But in the hunt for new customers, Mallya, who has had little involvement with the game, underestimated the importance of the traditional followers of the game.

The Royal Challengers were dealt a fatal blow on the first day of IPL by Kolkata Knight Riders, and the Kiwi wicketkeeper Brendon McCullum in particular, who smashed a T20 record of 158 runs off 73 balls. Since it was IPL's opening match, and held in Bangalore, Mallya left no stone unturned to live up to his carefully-crafted image of 'The King of Good Times'.

'In all fairness to Mallya, the show he put up for the opening day was truly mind-boggling. It was almost as if he was throwing a personal party for the 40,000 spectators in the stadium. The fireworks display, the grand cultural performances and the massive scale of everything around that night's show was simply world class. Members of the foreign media ran short of adjectives to describe the grand spectacle,' remembered a close associate of Mallya.

However, halfway through the fourteen matches that a team had to play, Royal Challengers was anchored to the bottom of the table, and the manner of its defeats did not offer any glimmer of hope for better performances in the future, making Mallya and his expensively-assembled team a butt of cricket jokes.

The dismal showing became more of an embarrassment for the honorary doctorate in business administration from University of South California, who used the marketing might of his UB Group. UB's top brass was pressed into full-time IPL service with senior executives, including the company's president Vijay Rekhi, in attendance at all the matches – at home and away.

In a desperate attempt to stop the team's free fall, Mallya sacked the Royal Challengers' CEO, Charu Sharma, amidst speculation that the captain Dravid too might step down along with Coach Venkatesh Prasad.

'My biggest mistake was to abstain from the selection of the team. Though I watch a lot of cricket whenever possible, I am no expert at the end of the day. I had a separate list of players that I wanted. But since Dravid is such an iconic player, I trusted his judgement. And Charu Sharma also backed him completely,' said Mallya.

'Unfortunately in cricket, unlike in any other sport, the captain is the boss,' he added wistfully. His personal wish list, which was discarded into the dustbin, apparently had the names of Dhoni, Robin Uthappa (he got him in the trade before the start of the second season) and Brendon McCullum (who was responsible for the first-match thrashing of Bangalore).

Charu Sharma, the ousted CEO was flummoxed with the manner of Mallya's sudden outburst. 'I look at the mirror every morning and wonder why I was considered inadequate. I have no clue about why things happened this way. Mallya listened to Dravid, who was responsible for choosing the team. No team is perfect. But did we get the team we wanted? No. The key players were missing at key times,' Sharma said. Thankfully for Mallya, this was IPL, and not EPL, where the financial implications of finishing at the bottom are massive. The bottom three teams in the English football league are relegated to a lower division and lose out something close to $100 million each from television broadcast rights. Apart from a few weeks of adverse publicity, and loss of face, Mallya didn't stand to lose much monetarily at the end of the season. 'I know I have a huge fan base and I have let them down. But give me one year, and we will be the winners,' Mallya said.

The trouble with Royal Challengers epitomized the classical clash between cricket and corporate cultures. Having pumped in millions of dollars, Mallya wanted results. A corporate icon, who hates to lose, he wanted to win at any cost. And he thought that with his money and management talent pool, he could pull this off too. Royal Challengers would be a winner just like his whiskey and beer brands.

The apocryphal stories are that Mallya's managers didn't understand why they couldn't win on the cricket field the way they won in the market place. Why weren't their corporate strategies working on the ground? Hence, they blamed the players, CEO and coach of the team.

Unlike in business, where marginal increase in sales, or reduced losses, in a quarter can be a cause for optimism, in a format of sport such as T20, only victory matters. If franchise owners didn't understand cricket culture, it was too early for cricketers to be mindful of the pressure on managers, and its impact on the decision making.

After all, it was the first time in India that players were directly answerable to someone who paid their salaries. If Kerry Packer could walk into the West Indies dressing room during his rebel World Series Cricket days, and blast a team comprising Viv Richards, Clive Lloyd, and Andy Roberts for poor performance, why would Mallya and Ambani put up with insipid performances?

Midway through the league, when nothing was going its way, the Royal Challengers decided to stick to the original schedule of taking a break during the period when they had no matches to play. A trip to Ranthambore had been planned earlier, and thirty rooms booked for the players and the coaching staff at the Taj Resort there.

But because the team had lost several matches, the managers at UB saw no reason why the team should be going on a holiday. 'How can the team members go on a holiday while they are losing so many matches? Shouldn't they use this time to practice harder and strategize better so that they can win the future matches? What is the kind of message that this holiday will send within the hierarchy? At UB, we work doubly hard if we fail to meet our beer sales targets. Cricketers should do the same,' a senior manager told the CEO of the team and other members.

Taking the cudgels on players' behalf, Charu Sharma, who was still the team's CEO, argued that international cricketers couldn't be treated like mules. 'Do you think the team is losing deliberately? Do you think any bowler loves being hit for a six, or a batsman getting out for a duck?' was his poser. Ultimately, the managers prevailed and the trip was cancelled.

'Cricket and business are different. Anything could happen on a given day on a cricket field. You could lose one day, and win the next one. Winning and losing is part of cricket. But the UB managers thought differently,' lamented a Royal Challenger player. Moreover, according to a team insider, Dravid's aloofness didn't help matters. 'Dravid didn't intervene or act as a buffer between the cricketers and the managers. As the team's icon player and respected cricketer, he had the stature to do so. He also had a direct line to Mallya to sort these things out. But he didn't. Maybe he was too afraid, too distant, or just too interested in the money,' he said.

Business executives might have got away bullying the 'salaried' players, but when you take on cricket administrators and board officials in India, it's a lopsided bout, no matter how big the company's balance sheet. Many franchises realized this fairly quickly and sought the services of men well acquainted with the babudom of Indian cricket.

Delhi Daredevils, for instance, sought the services of Amrit Mathur, a BCCI-appointed manager for the Indian team on numerous overseas tours, and seasoned sports administrator with several other bodies, including the Delhi Commonwealth Games organizing committee, to iron out logistics and infrastructure issues at the city's Feroz Shah Kotla Stadium. Mathur also helped the franchise deal with various civic agencies in the city and the local police during the matches.

Here too, Mallya's managers lost the plot. According to a few officials of the Karnataka State Cricket Association, UB executives acted as if they owned the stadium, the cricketers and the association itself after buying the city's IPL franchise.

'Mallya's managers started ordering the KSCA officials, and wanted them to implement changes inside the stadium according to their wishes. They wanted a special enclosure here, a newly erected platform there, and basically UB banners everywhere. They were in for a shock when the association asked them to get lost,' said a team insider.

Better sense did prevail in the end as UB managers backed-off in the confrontation, and Brijesh Patel, the influential KSCA supremo, was appointed Sharma's successor as the team CEO, with an eye on helping to ease the infrastructure niggles. Will Mallya learn other lessons in the second season?

skips, slips and sighs

It was a billion dollar gamble that paid off. It was a soap opera with several twists and turns, and a climax that was better than a Bollywood or Hollywood flick. An experience of several lifetimes, crunched in those forty-odd days, it panned out exactly the way Shane Warne, the 'best captain Australia never had', had predicted. His opening words at the Rajasthan Royals' first get-together were: 'Come on boys, join me. This is going to be fun, an experience. Who wants to jump on board?' In retrospect, every player in the victorious team did – and had fun all the way to the championship.

But then anyone who knows the legendary leg spinner – or the greatest player cricket has ever seen, according to some – can tell you that Warne is a compulsive gambler. Agreed Tom Moody, the former Australian cricketer and currently the coach of Mohali's Kings XI Punjab: 'He is a great gambler, who makes everyone believe that he's got all the aces. That's how he pulls off these million dollar bets. I wasn't in the least surprised with what he did to the Rajasthan Royals. He gave everyone, most importantly his teammates and the opposition teams, the impression that he was 2-3 balls ahead in the game with a little field change here and there. If Rahul Dravid or Yuvraj Singh, or any other captain in the IPL had done the same things, he would have been criticized. But when it came to Warne, these moves were considered to be strokes of a genius. That's the magic of Warne.'

In past several interviews, Warne has lamented that his life has been a 'soap opera'. Consider this: here is a living legend, a genius, who almost f***ed up his cricketing career by getting involved with the cricket-betting mafia, and who has been embroiled in several on- and off-field verbal brawls with other cricketers. At a personal level, his wife left him, and his name has been linked with several women. As Paul Barry wrote in a Warne biography (*Spun Out: Shane Warne: The Unauthorized Biography of a Cricketing Genius*): 'He has stripped naked and begged one woman for sex, the tabloids have told us, bombarded another with text messages saying "I can't wait to fuck you", and urged a third to seduce his wife into a threesome, which he said might save his marriage.'

Since his school days, Warne has been a truant, a boy who refused to grow up. Cut back to Barry's biography: 'Two decades later, his school mates say he was like any other young lad whose hormones were running hot. Yet none seems surprised by the trouble he now gets himself into. Twenty years on, they say, he has not grown up. He's still a big kid. He acts first and thinks later. Or as his headmaster Bob Hutchings puts it: "He's no different now to what he was aged eighteen. He was always a lover of life and a lover of women. He was fairly hedonistic then, he did what he wanted and never thought about the consequences. I don't think he's changed."' Meet the real Mister (Master) Shane Warne.

However, this Mister is truly a master on the cricket field. In fact, controversies and complications energize him to perform better – to give that extra tweak to his fingers, spin a yard more, flip it faster, and straighten-out more batsmen. As Barry puts it: 'His resilience in the face of such disgrace is a marvel. Shane … seems to be thriving on the attention. He is playing better than ever. Maybe he likes the limelight, whatever its source. Or maybe he just doesn't care. Maybe, both are true. Maybe, the child in him never lets him die as a great cricketer.'

This dichotomy brings us to the first of the several myths, which were freely propagated about Warne, after he catapulted Rajasthan Royals to an unexpected, shocking, unbelievable, and dramatic win in the first IPL tournament. The Jaipur team was the minnow, the David pitted against seven Goliaths. It had no heroes, except Warne (and possibly Graeme Smith, South African captain and part of the Rajasthan Royals team), who had hung up his international boots over a year ago. It had no hope, nothing to play for, or look forward to. Rumours were that Rajasthan Royals was in IPL solely for one reason: the *benami* or proxy promoter of the team was the architect of IPL, Lalit Modi, and that the 'public' promoters were connected to him.

When Warne and his team won, the accolades wouldn't stop. Everyone who knew anything about cricket called him a strategist who could out-think anyone on the cricket field, a captain par excellence who could charge his not-so-exceptional team members to perform better than the best, and a motivator who, said his former Australian teammate Moody, provided 'calm and sometime inspirational leadership'. The apocryphal stories that flowed out of the Jaipur team's dugouts would leave you in no doubt that Warne was a bleach-blonde incarnation of Sun Tzu (who wrote *The Art of War* centuries ago) with a distinct Australian twang.

For those who couldn't decipher his tactics, he became the 'mystery' man. Most couldn't understand his recipe and resorted to hyperbole while describing his leadership qualities. According to one blogger:

'The best model for this form (T20) of the game is the Rajasthan Royals' model. A lot of high potential fringe players who have everything to prove and nothing to lose. An icon like Warne at the helm puts even a Graeme Smith secure in his role. Warne is canny, street smart, tactically on the ball. He knows every player inside out, their strengths, their roles ... he throws them into the deep end and expects them to do well. And they respond.

'How he infuses confidence in the younger lot is something I would dearly love to know but I know this much – he will not do it quietly like Dhoni ... All fringe players know their role, know their captain knows how to use them, all senior players with well defined roles again, and at the very top, Warne using the power of his personality, his understanding of human nature, the game of cricket and what it takes to get the slightest of advantages and translate that into a win.'

Others ascribed tactical traits and thinking to Warne's captaincy. Here's how another blogger described the nature of Pakistan's team if Warne hypothetically became the country's coach.

'Warne would believe that he needs regular openers and not part timers. You see any world-class team; they have had regular strong openers ... Warne also chose regular openers in IPL. Swapnil Asnodkar and Smith regularly provided excellent starts. So, I would guess that Warne would use regular openers for Pakistan ... Warne loves to pick players who are relatively unknown and make them heroes. This generates a sense of respect for him. Asnodkar is an example ... Warne is famous for giving roles to his players, as if he is Shakespeare directing Hamlet ... !'

It was impossible, even for Warne to remain unaffected by such praises. In one of his several interviews during IPL season one, Warne had this to say about his strategy, 'Some people had branded us underdogs but we had self belief, we worked out some plans and executed them ... It would also mean that we will have to work out new strategies. The surprise element plays a big role in this form of cricket. We did apply this strategy by asking Yusuf Pathan and Dinesh Salunkhe to bowl. The other teams have started copying our strategy but with new players coming in we too will have to think over again. They can be dangerous too. We will have basics covered and work out plans.'

ICON BY INSTINCT

Such an emphasis on pre-match strategy and planning is exactly what the impulsive Warne hated when he was playing for the

Australian squad. He knows the craft, but he takes his decisions on the field, he thinks on his feet. One can't imagine Warne sitting in front of a video footage for hours to figure out how to get Tendulkar or Dravid out. He will just walk on to the field with his mischievous smile, roll up his sleeves, and deliver six different balls. And if he hasn't made an impact, he will deliver another six variations in the second over. If that doesn't work either, he will just bowl the 'ball of the century' that's simply unplayable.

Listen to him carefully, and often enough you are most likely to walk away with the same feeling. He once said during IPL that 'to me, a captain must run the show. You train hard and then get out and play. In Rajasthan, if we had a day off there were no meetings or any of that rubbish. If people needed to go to the gym or wanted a session in the pool that was their business.' After thumping the Delhi Daredevils by 105 runs in the semi-finals, he felt that 'some days your tactics come off. The players were up for it and you could tell that from our intensity on the field. It was still not our best game and I hope we have saved it for the final.'

When Rajasthan Royals won the finals on the last ball, he gave another insight into his instinctive style of captaincy. 'I am a believer in fate, and I just knew we were destined to win that final. We'd won three or four games off the last ball or in the last over and I thought, We're meant to win this. So I was relaxed as we got to the last ball and still needed a run to win. Sohail Tanvir was on strike. I said, "Whatever happens, watch the ball, swing as hard as you possibly can and then run fast." "Skipper," he said, "I'm going to do this for you." It was a pretty amazing thing to hear.'

Now, let's for the moment, simply deconstruct this one paragraph. Like Hindu Indians, Warne seems to be a believer in destiny. And if you go through his cricketing career, nothing else can explain why he did what he did, unless you give the wheel-of-fortune a huge swing. He wanted to be a rugby player, like all young 'studs' in Australian schools and colleges, and not a cricketer. He could have easily been chucked out of school teams. He nearly lost his place in the junior teams and none of the established coaches wanted to touch him. It was Lady Luck who helped him find one who decided to.

His coach, Terry Jenner was a has-been and an alcoholic. But he turned out to be exactly the kind of mentor that a truant Warne needed.

More importantly, Warne could have easily become a 5-tests cricketer like hundreds of others in Australia. Yet again, it was the 'gambling' trait in his captain that enabled him to stay in the national side. In his first few tests, Warne nearly went wicketless and gave away many runs. By the time he played in that test against Sri Lanka, his self-confidence was possibly at the lowest ebb. He even went to some of his colleagues and admitted that he was probably not cut out for the Australian side.

Then came the turning point in his cricketing career. The Sri Lankans were 6 for 137 in their second innings, needing a few more runs to win. Alan Border, the brilliant Australian captain, chucked the ball to Warne. The leg spinner couldn't believe his eyes or brains. Had Border gone mad? He thought the move was suicidal considering the manner in which he had bowled in the first innings or the previous tests. As far as Warne knew, the game would be over in a few overs if he was allowed to bowl. But he got a wicket at that crucial juncture. Then he got another one. And a third. Australia had won. In a jiffy, Warne was on a short run-up to become one of the world's greatest cricketer – and possibly the best spinner.

Now let's go back to what he told Tanvir, who faced the last ball in the finals – 'Watch the ball, swing hard, and run fast'. That's quintessential Warne. There are no complications in his strategy or approach. There is no tactical thinking such as placing the last ball where there were open spaces, or hitting it towards a particular fielder who's slow, or tapping the ball lightly to make way for an easy single. It's simple and straightforward – watch, swing and run. And leave the rest to chance.

This was true about his bowling too. If he was going to bowl a leg spinner, it had to turn a mile. If it was a flipper bowled from the front of the hand, it had to skid – and skid fast. If it was a top spinner, it had to jump. And he would bowl wherever there were roughs, even if they were two feet away from the leg stump. From there, he could turn the ball sharp enough to hit the off stump. That was the bottom line for Warne. All the other things were minor variations.

THE URGE TO BE LIKED

Now for the final part of the conversation the Rajasthan Royals' captain had with his No 11 batsman, Tanvir. This time, it was Tanvir who said that he would win the game just for his skipper. This is yet another side to Warne as a cricketer, and more so as a captain. It is his ability to earn respect and love of his teammates. Warne can goad people to give 100 per cent on the field.

Excuse me, you would say, but isn't that what captaincy is all about? Isn't that how Ganguly and Ponting became great captains? Yet again, please read our words carefully. We never said that Warne is not a good leader. All we said was that he is not a strategist. Even his trait to extract the best out of his players, to make them die rather than fail, only proves it.

First, one needs to establish the reasons why Warne feels compelled to be liked by others. Warne's coach Jenner thought that there were other layers beneath Warne's seemingly super-confident attitude. As Barry explained in his book: 'He (Jenner) could see something else too, behind the bravado, that many people missed, and this was the insecurity that is so obvious in Warne today. He desperately wanted people to like him, to praise him, to say how good he was. "Why is he like that?" asks Jenner, "I don't know. Maybe that's the way he's made."'

Even if they don't start that way, insecurity is the fate of almost every leg spinner, Jenner believes, because their daily experience encourages self-doubt. 'You're told not to bring your girlfriend to the game because she'll go off with the fast bowler. Then your dad and mum come down and you don't get a bowl. And if you are brought on, all the other parents go and sit in front of their windscreens. It's the same with your teammates

… No one believes in you. That's what every leg spinner has to endure.'

Later, as you become famous, the urge to be liked slowly transforms into a conviction that you have to be liked. So, there's a constant interplay between the two: the inherent insecurity forces you to act in a manner so as to be loved by others, and the conviction rejects those who don't love you as you feel that you deserve the love.

In his book, Barry says, 'But just close your eyes for a second and stand in his shoes, and try to get a glimpse of what it is like to be him. You're the best in the world at the one thing that matters to you. You're cheered by the crowd as you run onto the pitch, feted by teammates again and again. You're mobbed by women wherever you go. Is it any wonder that you think the world revolves around you?

'You're incredibly vain. You love to be loved … Psychologists call it "entitlement", the feeling that you deserve it, you've earned it, it's your due, your reward.

'As one who has worked with the Australian cricket team describes it: "You get so famous that you think you're bigger than Ben Hur. You're entitled to this and entitled to that and no one can tell you anything. Warne will only listen to people that he thinks can help him go somewhere. He shies away from control, authority or demands for rational behaviour." In its extreme form this syndrome is a mental illness called narcissistic personality disorder; Warne appears to be suffering a milder version.'

Therefore, throughout the IPL, one witnessed these twin emotions in Warne's captaincy. He went out of his way to be loved by his teammates, and he rejected everything that didn't fit in his scheme of things.

One of the most important things that Warne did was to make his teammates feel that they were in a non-stop party during IPL's first season. They were there to have fun, and the results didn't have any meaningful consequences. And Warne just didn't voice these sentiments; he led by example by doing the same whether he was holidaying on a Goa beach before an important game, or having several glasses of beer after an unexpected victory.

It started from day one with Warne's opening words during the first get-together of the Rajasthan Royals team. They were not exactly some Churchilian exhortation of troops or a Sun Tzu exultation of victory cries. Nor were they the words of a strategist or a tactician.

Similarly, just before the grand and glitzy finals in Mumbai, there wasn't a huddle, a team motto, or setting of 'targets'. Amidst the distraction of fireworks, deafening music, and the ceremonial speechmaking, all that Warne had to say to his players was: 'Boys, we don't know whether this entire group will be together again. Let's make sure tonight is the one of the best nights of our life.'

So, how would you now encapsulate his leadership skills? We would compare his management skills to that of a CEO during the heady boom days in the New Economy sector in the US Silicon Valley. Warne created an atmosphere like the one that was prevailing within the thousands of dotcoms and dozens of venture capital firms sprinkled across the Valley in the late 1990s.

Almost every VC, founder, co-founder or CEO in the Net-related business during that period was having fun. He/she had an idea, there was enough funding available, and he/she managed to attract similar-thinking people and walked together into a never-ending party. And who else captured this environment better than Po Bronson, author of *Nudist on the Late Shift*. Here are a few glimpses from Bronson's never-to-be-used script for a movie.

Here's how people were offered jobs – by strangers.

Dion: Think about it, Stowe. Come work for us.

Stowe: You're kidding, right. Did June put you up to this?

Dion: I'm not kidding. We should talk more. Banking's a dinosaur, anyway.

Stowe: But you don't know anything about me.

Dion: Studies show you make your mind up about people in the first minute, no matter what you learn later.

Stowe: Are you pulling my leg? You haven't even told me what you do.

Money and opportunity came unexpectedly.

Ho: I want in.

Lori: Want in what?

Ho: Significant-other.com. I heard all about it. One of the judges at the club is a scout for me.

Lori: You're kidding.

Ho: It'll be a great companion to the investment I have in Wedding Planner.

Lori: Look, Ho, you know, I was up there just as a prank, really. Just floating a balloon. I'm not serious.

Ho: Afraid to admit you'd really like to do it because "what if you failed", huh?

This gets her. Maybe he is right.

Lori: You'd really consider investing in me?

Ho: In a second. I know you. I trust you.

Finally, this is how people took decisions to chuck up their jobs and start on their own.

Stowe: We've got a great life in New York. Would we really throw that away to move out here on a whim?

Lori: We could keep the apartment. The lease allows us to sublet it for a year.

Stowe: You don't think we are too late? I mean, how long can the boom last?

Lori: Every year we say that. And every year the boom continues.

Stowe: Maybe you're right. We'd be crazy not to try this.

In the case of Rajasthan Royals, Warne convinced his teammates that they were on the winning pitch. Almost every team member is sure that it was Warne who created the environment for the fabulous performances. The Aussie did what few skippers have been able to.

So, did Warne walk on water? 'He most certainly did and made fifteen others do it as well,' felt Fraser Castellino, the former CEO of Rajasthan Royals, who has now moved to Bangalore. 'Shane asked his players to walk on the edge, game after game and told them even if they were to falter he was there to hold them. There are many captains who would say this, but Warne led by example in that match against Deccan Chargers and even the finals.'

Against Deccan Chargers, who scored 214 for 5 wickets in their 20 overs, everyone thought that the Hyderabad team had posted enough runs to register its first win in the IPL tournament. Only they didn't realize that Warney boy had other plans. Needing 17 runs for victory in the final over, Warne hit a four and two crispy sixers off the bowling of Andrew Symonds to shatter Deccan Chargers' dream.

THE NEAR-PERFECT CAPTAIN

In dealing with team members, Warne became a near-perfect captain, said Castellino, 'for the younger, immature players such as Ravindra Jadeja, Asnodkar, and Yusuf Pathan, whose game was built on unpredictability and a bit of fearlessness.'

Throughout the tournament, Warne kept talking up his bunch of youngsters who weren't even first choice players for their state teams. In post-match interviews, he singled out players such as Siddharth Trivedi, Jadeja and Niraj Patel as good enough to represent India. He named the twenty-four-year-old leg spinner Dinesh Salunkhe, who earned his right to be part of the Rajasthan Royals thanks to a television talent hunt conducted by the franchise promoters as India's best spin hope. Now Salunkhe hadn't played a single first class game, and was not even part of any Ranji team. After nicknaming him 'magician', Warne would tell Tanvir, 'When the ball is in your hand, think you are the best bowler on the earth.'

Many of the Rajasthan Royals' players too couldn't stop

showering praises for their skipper. After Team Jaipur's success, Pathan said that Warne was a 'great teacher. He has absolutely no airs and is always going out of his way to help and share the tricks of the trade. He is not only our captain and coach but is also our friend and guide, which is why she has been successful in getting the best out of every single player. They say a good captain should be two overs ahead of the game and Warne is just that. He is always thinking, outrageously positive and thrives under pressure. He is indeed the team's pride and joy.'

Even the Rajasthan Royals' chairman and co-owner, Manoj Badale, described Warne's captaincy in terms of emotional phrases. 'His style of leadership makes an owner's job much easier. He has an extraordinary personality, and brings a charisma and enjoyment to the whole camp. He brings out the best in all individuals, and even makes support staff feel 20 per cent more confident. He is a generous man, and expects the same for him – as his team gets.'

What was surprising was that a player like Smith, who has often been involved in verbal spats with Warne in both the international and English county matches couldn't stop lavishing praises on Captain Warne.

After the Royals won the semi-finals, Smith told reporters that 'as a captain, there is so much to learn from him, just by observing how he prepares before a match, how he thinks about the game and how he motivates his boys. He makes everyone in the team feel good about themselves. I'm just twenty-seven, so there was plenty for me to learn in there.' Players from the opposing teams, who partied with the youngsters in the Rajasthan Royals' team, admitted that 'before the match, Warne would walk up to each player and tell him how his performance would be the most crucial and decisive.'

This was the secret behind Warne's success. His ability to make every player feel more important than the others, his focus on letting the players enjoy themselves and his instinctive thinking. Here are a few examples of his decision-making process during the matches.

In one of his interviews, Warne said that 'in T20 competition, we try to do different plans for every game depending on the wickets. We don't use computers. We use our brains.' And whenever things haven't gone according to any short-term plan, Warne has changed them. Said one of the players in the team: 'Our first game didn't go according to plan. In a funny sort of a way, it helped us. Some strategies we had didn't work, and we said look, this is what happens and then we got it right in the next game.'

In fact, after the first game, Warne's captaincy went into an overdrive. No one really knew – or even guessed – what he would do on the field. So, in the match against Deccan Chargers on 9 May 2008, Munaf Patel, the fast bowler, bowled unchanged and got a wicket in his third over. Just eleven days later, in the game against the Kolkata Knight Riders, Warne bowled three different bowlers in the first three overs – Tanvir, Patel, and Shane Watson. The fourth was bowled by Tanvir again, but from the opposite end. This constant change of bowlers helped, as the Kolkata team 'struggled to settle down' and scored only 50 runs in the first 10 overs.

Warne himself took charge of the bowling in many games, coming in on early to set the tempo, or change it. Against Deccan Chargers, he boldly bowled the seventh over and finished with a credible 2-20, claiming the wickets of the two most dangerous batsmen – Adam Gilchrist and Shahid Afridi.

More importantly, Warne managed to get the team to be together. It was easy for him too; apart from South African Smith, he was clearly the most respected member of the team.

At the start of IPL, Chennai's captain Dhoni had predicted that whichever team gels better would win the tournament. And as the season progressed, Warne's team was definitely the best in this regard. As one of the Jaipur's players told a newspaper: 'He isn't a control freak but the only thing he asks for is effort. In case one does that, there are no complaints.' Another newspaper described the Jaipur team possessing 'youthful exuberance and adrenalin charge'. A third said that a game for the team was like a 'walk in the park'.

WARNE THE BUILDER

There is one telling incident that indicates the kind of team that Warne built around him.

On 30 May 2008, the Royals played their semi-finals against the Daredevils. The young Swapnil Asnodkar walked in to open the Royals' innings with the young, but more experienced, Smith. And here's how one newspaper described the initial part of the game.

'Early in the Rajasthan Royals innings, one couldn't help but smile when Asnodkar ran across from the non-striker's end to have a chat with fellow-opener Smith, who was struggling with his dodgy hamstring and dicey timing. The pint-sized Asnodkar, whose normal gaze would reach the burly 6-foot-plus Smith's navel, tilted his head more than 45 degrees to utter quick words of encouragement to his troubled mate.

'... Smith had been in charge of one of the best ODI outfits in the world and a long-standing skipper of a very successful test side but today he was getting words of advice from a rank junior with no international experience. But things were different today. At the time the conversation was taking place, Asnodkar had hit four fours while Smith just had one.

'About three hours later, when Warne was once again swarmed by his committed worker-bees to signal Rajasthan Royals' Warne-inspired semi-final victory, one understood the seriousness of that light-hearted moment at the start of the innings. There are no commoners in the Royals squad.

'Asnodkar didn't worry about Smith's pedigree and treated him like just another teammate.'

This was the beauty of Warne and Royals. He was the over-riding authority that no one questioned, and his boys felt, thought, and played like a team. Every member was an equal, with Warne being more equal than others.

1983 TO 2008

Writing about the success of the Portland basketball team in the US NBA league, David Halberstam, in his book *The Breaks of the Game*, observed: 'But basketball was far more vulnerable to the change caused by the arrival of big money. For basketball demanded that though the players be talented, they also subordinate their individual talents to the idea of team and to each other. A truly great basketball player was not necessarily someone who scored a lot of points; a truly great basketball player was someone of exceptional talent and self-discipline who could make his teammates better.'

This is exactly what happened with the Jaipur team. The players played – and covered – for each other. No one was interested in his own statistics; only the team mattered. They became unselfish and less egoistic. In some ways, it reminded us of the victorious Kapil's Devils in 1983 (ODI World Cup), and Dhoni's Daredevils in 2007 (T20 World Cup).

Neither of these two teams had stars. Everyone in both the teams gave match-winning performances at least once during the two tournaments. There were several players who chipped in at regular intervals with critical batting, bowling or fielding performances. Someone or the other lifted his game in a match or two. And everyone had to be credited with the victories in the two tournaments. Like Warne, Kapil led from the front. His scintillating knock against Zimbabwe, when India was tottering at 17 for 5, was the first giant step towards the Cup.

For Dhoni & Co., the turning point in the T20 World Cup came after a lost game. Ironically, while Kapil's boys picked up steam after winning a nearly-lost game against Zimbabwe, Dhoni's men became a team after they lost from a near-win position against New Zealand. It was after this match that India realized that she could win against a better team; she had the capability and the skills to achieve it. Then, there was no stopping for India as it strode from one victory to another to lift the T20 Cup.

What is surprising about all these three victories – India in 1983 and 2007, and Rajasthan Royals in 2008 – is that all the three captains were unexpected choices. Kapil has admitted that he never wanted to be the skipper, the choice of Dhoni's was controversial, and Warne was not exactly meant to be one.

WAS HE THE CHOSEN ONE?

In fact, Warne was never the over-riding original choice for the captaincy of the Jaipur team. Badale made it clear during an exclusive e-mail interview with us. 'Warne's views could only be factored in after the first (players') auction, and it is clear, given the choice of Graeme Smith, that we did not build a team around Warne. But rather, we picked a team based on individual roles and records.'

Badale added that the promoters did have 'extensive meetings with Warne in London, ahead of the auction to discuss his role as captain and coach – an approach that he was very keen to take. It was never a precondition, but a preference.'

However, it can be argued here that Rajasthan Royals had no choice in the matter. They couldn't bank upon Warne because they were never sure whether they would be able to buy him. After all, anything can happen in a players' auction.

The same is true about 'picks' or 'drafts' in American baseball league. In a 2003 book, *Moneyball*, the author Michael Lewis discussed the fears and apprehensions that surround a baseball team that has to pick players up in a pre-decided order.

'The A's (Oakland Athletics) front office has a list, never formally written out, of the twenty players they'd draft in a perfect world. That is, if money were no object and twenty-nine other teams were not also vying to draft the best amateur players in the country. The list is a pure expression of the new view of amateur players. On it are eight pitchers and twelve hitters – all for the moment, just names.

'... Of the players on his list he could afford, and stood any chance of getting, Billy (A's coach) thinks he might land as many as six. But the truth is he doesn't know. It was possible he'd only get one of the players on the wish list. By the time the A's made their second pick, the twenty-fourth of the draft, all of them might be gone.' In that year, before the 2002 season began, the A's 'had nabbed, incredibly thirteen players: four pitchers and nine hitters', from their wish list.

One of the CEOs at the IPL's first players' auction maintained that the same was true in this case. 'Every IPL franchise had a wish list, but no one got what it wanted. No one's strategy at team selection worked.' Many of the globally renowned players like Australians Glen McGrath and Simon Katich, and West Indian Shivnaraine Chanderpaul went into the bin thrice as no team was interested in buying them. It was just Dame Fortune who played the key role.

The auction process was simple. Names of the various players would be taken out of the bin, and the teams would be asked to bid for each one. The minimum bid had to start at the pre-decided base price. But if no one bid for the player, the name would go back into the bin to be taken out later. So, in the case of the above-mentioned cricketers, no one bid the first time. In some cases, none of the teams bid for a few players for as many as three times.

If others, who were present at the auction, are to be believed, Jaipur was not really interested in Warne. It was more serious about building a team around Smith, a young and aggressive captain, who would have been an ideal theoretical choice to lead the other young players that Jaipur bid for.

Here's an apocryphal story told to us by a team CEO, who was present at the auction.

'Warne's was one of the first names that came up, as the seventy-eight players (who were auctioned initially) names were picked up. But no one was willing to pick him up at the reserve price. There was no response from any of the teams for seconds, even more than a minute. The auction was headed for a disaster within the first few minutes. A player of Warne's capability was unsellable. Since Modi has some interest in the Jaipur team (*see* ch. *IPl or ICL* on IPL controversies), he made an eye contact with Badale & Co., and nudged them to start the bidding. Jaipur raised the placard, probably to only kick start the process, hoping other teams would jump into the fray. This would start the bidding on a good note to Modi's satisfaction. But no other team bid for Warne. Jaipur, it seemed, was saddled with Warne. No one knows for sure whether Jaipur really wanted him, taking into account the initial hesitancy; it just had to buy the legendary, but retired, leg spinner.'

If this story is true, even to some extent, it would imply that Jaipur, as Badale hinted, never wanted to build a team around Warne. It was just forced to do so later.

GETTING THEM CHEAP

Similarly, Badale claims that Jaipur focused on the second players' auction, as it wanted to buy lesser known, but highly talented, younger players at lower prices. The reason: the strategy was to choose an ideal combination at the lowest possible price. This is why the Jaipur team bid for very few international players realizing that only four of them could play in any XI, and focused on cheaper local talent in the second round. But this too may be a just a thought in retrospect.

Many teams contend that there was never supposed to be a second round. Badale maintains that he was sure that there would be a second round. However, one of the teams' CEO is adamant that the second round was forced later for a unique reason.

'Immediately after the first round of players' auction, the teams started talking to the various players in the India U-19 team. Since there was suddenly a demand as "younger" slots had to be filled up in each team, the U-19 players realized that there were attractive opportunities for them if they played their cards in the right manner. They knew that they could earn unbelievable money.

'This led to competition. One of the younger players agreed to play for a team at a certain amount, but then came back and said that his fee needs to be hiked. The reason: one of his teammates, who wasn't in the regular U-19 XI, was being paid more by another team. Similarly, another player asked the IPL franchises to get in touch with his agent. And all this was happening while the U-19 team was playing the junior World Cup tournament, which it subsequently won.

'When the BCCI president Pawar got to know about these incidents, he immediately put a stop to such negotiations. He asked the players to focus on the World Cup, and asked all the franchises not to speak to any of the players. So, once the U-19 World Cup was over, something had to be done about these players. There were a few New Zealanders and other international players, who too had evinced an interest in IPL and they too had to be adjusted among the eight teams. It was then that the IPL Committee decided on a second auction.'

How were the sixteen players, who represented India in the U-19 World Cup, distributed among the various teams? 'In this case, the American NBA model was followed. The names of all the franchises were put into a lottery box, and the first chit got to pick up the first pick. But because this team had the first choice, it was forced to make the second pick as the last one. The second chit made the second pick and the second last one. And so on and so forth.' Therefore, it was quite difficult – almost impossible – for any team to follow a selection strategy in this process. No one could, not even Rajasthan Royals.

To see how luck mattered, here are a few examples from the second auction. In this round, Delhi Daredevils got the first chance to pick up a player. Bangalore's Royal Challengers, who had its eyes set on Virat Kohli, thought it could never get him. Kohli was a Delhi lad, and Daredevils were sure to pick him up. Surprise, surprise! Delhi chose a fast bowler. Luckily, Bangalore's name came second and they greedily picked up Kohli. Since Bangalore was now entitled to only a 15th pick, out of sixteen players, it got wicketkeeper Srivatsa Goswami who, in the final analysis, turned out to be the most valuable player among the younger crop. 'That's the irony of biddings and auctions.'

Therefore, it is clear that Rajasthan Royals had not much choice in picking up either its captain or the younger players, if others are to be believed.

In fact, the truth is that it did not even get some of the mainstream players, who were in its wish list. If one goes by the events at the first players' auction, it demolishes another myth about Rajasthan Royals: that it deliberately and strategically bid for players, available at low prices and, therefore, saved money.

In contrast, Jaipur was prepared to spend upto a million dollar for a player.

Take the case of Ishant Sharma, India's fast bowler, whose bidding witnessed an intensity that was seen only in the case of world-class Australian players like Gilchrist and Symonds. Initially, it was Hyderabad versus Kolkata versus Jaipur. As the bidding reached around $600,000, the fight was between SRK and Badale.

When Jaipur said $625,000, Kolkata upped it to $650,000. Then it was $675,000 Jaipur, and the counter offer of $700,000 by King Khan. Jaipur took a break at that time, mulled over whether to hike its bid offer. There was a pregnant silence as Jaipur thought it over. $725,000. Kolkata $750,000. The Jaipur contingent went into a huddle again. SRK looked over at Rajasthan Royals' table and smiled. It was clear what he was thinking: surely, Jaipur didn't have the moneybags to match his. Surely, Jaipur wouldn't go over this price.

To everybody's and King Khan's surprise, Jaipur upped it to $775,000. Kolkata countered with $800,000. SRK smiled again. He had Ishant in his bag. But Jaipur was unwilling to give up. The bidding reached a crescendo as Jaipur priced Ishant at $925,000. Kolkata responded with $950,000. The Jaipur delegation looked tense. Badale was biting his nails, or rather his fingers. It was a moment for him and his partners.

Should Jaipur pay nearly a million dollar for a rookie Indian player, who had only recently hogged the limelight with his astounding bowling? Should the promoters pay so much for a youngster, when they had bagged more senior players for less than half the price? What about their strategy of paying low? However, it seemed as if Jaipur was not averse to paying even an exorbitant sum for some players.

As Jaipur mulled over its tactics, one could see Mohali's Preity Zinta laughing. She was enjoying this bidding war. She was also excited to know the outcome. This was a classical fight: between

David and Goliath, between strategy and moneybags, between an unknown entity and a celebrity. At some level, many in the auction room wanted Jaipur to beat SRK. And some of the superstar's friends, like Preity, wished that SRK would show Jaipur its real place.

Finally, the hammer went down. Kolkata had won. Ishant would play for SRK. Jaipur promoters knew they had tried their best and lost.

A similar thing happened during the bidding for Mohammad Kaif, a former Indian batsman, who was out of the national squad. But this one ended quite differently.

Yet again, the fight for Kaif was between Jaipur and Kolkata. The bid price reached $450,000 by Kolkata. Jaipur raised it to $475,000. Kolkata mulled over its next step. $500,000. $525,000. $550,000. The Jaipur contingent laughed. This was getting too much. But they raised the bid to $575,000. Kolkata $600,000.

Jaipur discussed its move now. On the Mohali table, Preity and Ness looked a bit bored, unlike their excitement later when the two teams were fighting over Ishant. Jaipur came back into the race. Kolkata responded with $650,000. Jaipur hiked it to $675,000. Kolkata thought Jaipur was paying too much for a non-national player and let Jaipur take him.

Both these examples show that it was only in retrospect that Jaipur gave the strategic logic that it deliberately paid less for players that it wanted in its team. This was not true. Rajasthan Royals was willing to pay huge amounts for some of the players. It was willing to pay nearly a million dollars for a player, which was among the highest in the first auction.

BASEBALL VS CRICKET

Another achievement of Badale and his co-promoters was that they based their team selection entirely on statistics. Badale compared his strategy to that of the Oakland A's, the American baseball team whose 2003 season is aptly described in Lewis' *Moneyball*. Badale had obviously read the book; during our conversation when we made a mistake and said that it was about the New York Yankees, he corrected us that it was actually about the A's.

Lewis claimed that he wrote the book because he fell in love with the story. 'The story concerned a small group of undervalued professional baseball players and executives, many of whom had been rejected as unfit for the big leagues, who had turned themselves into one of the most successful franchises in Major League Baseball.

'It began, really, with an innocent question: How did one of the poorest team in baseball, the Oakland Athletics, win so many games?

'For more than a decade, the people who run professional baseball have argued that the game was ceasing to be an athletic competition and becoming a financial one. The gap between the rich and poor in baseball was far greater than in any other professional sport, and widening rapidly. At the opening of the 2002 season, the richest team, the New York Yankees, had a payroll of $126 million while the two poorest teams, the Oakland A's and the Tampa Bay Devil Rays, had payrolls of less than a third of that ...

'For the past several years, working with either the lowest or next to lowest payroll in the game, the Oakland A's had won more regular season games than any other team, except the Atlanta Braves.

'At the bottom of the Oakland experiment was a willingness to rethink baseball: how it is managed, how it is played, who is best suited to play it, and why. Understanding that he would never have a Yankee-sized checkbook, the Oakland A's general manager, Billy Beane, had set about looking for inefficiencies in the game. Looking for, in essence, new baseball knowledge. In what amounted to a scientific investigation of their sport, the Oakland front office had reexamined everything from the market price of foot speed to the inherent difference between the average major league player and the superior Triple-A one. That's how they found their bargains. Many of the players drafted or acquired by the Oakland A's had been the victims of an unthinking prejudice rooted in baseball traditions.'

Like in the case of cricket, baseball managers and scouters invariably were biased towards those home run hitters, the players with bristling biceps and thighs, those who looked like natural athletes. The drafters or buyers never looked closely at records or statistics, or even the gap that they had to fill within their team. They looked at players who looked and felt good, no matter what they had done in the past few years as players. Any athlete can become a player, they thought.

But for Oakland A's Billy Beane, 'a young player is not what he looks like, or what he might become, but what he has done.' This logic was termed 'performance scouting', and it meant that 'most of what's important about a baseball player, maybe even including his character, can be found in his statistics.'

Therefore, the collection of statistics, and analyzing the right set of numbers, became the most critical part of Billy Beane's selection process. To that was added the requirements of the team, and not just getting a player whose stats were excellent.

There was another reason for this statistics-driven selection. It came in the form of a new kind of rich person named John Henry, who bought the Florida Marlins in January 1999. Most baseball owners were either heirs, or empire builders of one sort or another, or both. Henry had made his money in the intelligent end of the financial markets. He had an instinctive feel for the way statistical analysis could turn up inefficiencies in human affairs. Inefficiencies in the financial markets had made Henry a billionaire – and he saw some familiar idiocies in the market for baseball players.

'As Henry later wrote in a letter to ESPN's Rob Neyer: "People in both fields operate with beliefs and biases. To the extent you can eliminate both and replace them with data, you gain a clear advantage. Many people think they are smarter than others in the stock market and that the market itself has no intrinsic intelligence – as if it's inert. Many people think they are smarter than others in baseball and that the game on the field is simply what they think it is through their set of images/beliefs. Actual data from the market means more than individual perception/belief. The same is true in baseball.'"

Data and statistics had other advantages too, at least in baseball. 'Think about it. One absolutely cannot tell by watching, the difference between a .300 hitter and a .275 hitter. The difference is one hit every two weeks. It might be that a reporter, seeing every game that the team plays, could sense that difference over the course of the year if no records were kept, but I doubt it. Certainly the average fan, seeing perhaps a tenth of the team's games, could never gauge two performances that accurately ... The difference between a good hitter and an average hitter is simply not visible – it is a matter of record.'

In the case of Rajasthan Royals, Badale claims that he did the same thing in his selection process. The owners studied all the available records of the younger players, and talked extensively to their coaches. In the end, by statistically short-listing the players, they managed to create a winning team – and at a much lower cost. Just like the Oakland A's. What Billy was to baseball, Badale apparently was to T20.

However, there was a huge difference between Billy and Badale. This difference proves that while Billy's was a robust strategy, Badale's was plain luck.

The critical thing about Billy was that he reinterpreted all the available statistics about baseball. For example, 'no one in the big (baseball) league cares how often a college player walks; (Oakland A's) ... cares about it more than just about anything else. He doesn't explain why walks are important ... He doesn't explain that the important traits in a baseball player were not all equally important. That foot speed, fielding ability, even raw power tended to be dramatically overpriced. That the ability to control the strike zone was the greatest indicator of future success. That the number of walks a hitter drew was the best indicator of whether he understood how to control the strike zone.

'He doesn't explain that plate discipline might be an innate trait, rather than something a free-swinging amateur can be taught in the pros. He doesn't talk about all the other statistically based insights – the overwhelming importance of on-base percentage, the significance of pitches seen per plate appearance – that he uses to value precisely a hitter's contribution to a baseball offense.'

To further finesse the statistics, Oakland A's went a step further. The A's created its own statistical model. It took cue from AVM Systems, a company formed by two Wall Street derivatives experts, Ken Mauriello and Jack Armbruster. 'Ken analyzed the value of derivative securities, and Jack traded them for one of the more profitable Chicago trading firms. Their firm priced financial risk as finely as it had ever been priced. "In the late 1980s Kenny started looking at taking the same approach to major League baseball players," said Armbruster.'

Lewis describes the basis of the AVM model. 'There was hardly a play in baseball that, to be precisely valued, didn't need to be adjusted for the players involved, or the ballpark in which it occurred. What AVM's system really wanted to know was: in every event that occurs on a baseball field, how – and how much – should the players involved be held responsible, and therefore debited or credited?

'… how to account for a player's performance was obvious: runs. Runs were the money of baseball, the common denominator of everything that occurred on a field. How much each tiny event on a baseball field was worth was a more complicated issue. AVM dealt with it by collecting ten years of data from major league baseball games, of every ball that was put into play. Every event that followed a ball being put into play was compared by the system to what had typically happened during the previous ten years. "No matter what happens in a baseball game," said Armbruster, "it has happened thousands of times before." The performance of the players involved was always judged against the average.'

Once everything was recorded, the AVM system 'carved up what happened in every baseball game into countless, tiny, meaningful fragments. Derivatives. "There are all sorts of things that happen in the context of a baseball play," said Armbruster, "that just never got recorded." ... Just as it never occurred to anyone on Wall Street to think about the value of pieces of a stock or a bond until there was a pile of money to be made from the exercise, it never occurred to anyone in the market for baseball players to assign values to the minute components of a baseball player's performance – until baseball players became breathtakingly expensive.'

Now, if one has to take the Oakland A's model in the context of Rajasthan Royals, or cricket in general, one needs to go much beyond the statistics that are easily available.

For example, it would amount to judging a player like former Australian Michael Bevan in a totally different light. Instead of just looking at the runs he scored, his batting average, and his run rate, it would need to consider how many runs Bevan enabled his batting partners to score. Being an excellent runner between wickets, Bevan had this uncanny ability to convert ones into twos, twos into threes, even when his partner had hit the stroke. Is there any statistics about the runs that Bevan helped his partners to score? And shouldn't that be added to his batting performance?

As a counter logic, the new set of cricket statistics should tell us immediately how many runs Ganguly, a bad runner between wickets, missed. His overall batting average should include the singles that could have been taken, either by himself or his partners, but were not taken.

A similar thing should happen in the case of fielding. The South African Jonty Rhodes was a valuable player not only because of the runs he scored, but also because of the runs he saved at his position at point, or the unbelievable catches he took that changed the complexion of a match. Similar analysis should be done for Yuvraj Singh or Australia's Michael Clarke.

More importantly, what cricket statisticians need to do is to evaluate every single ball bowled in T20 matches, or ODIs and come up with a model that can predict how a certain player will behave in a given situation, or how a batsman would hit a certain ball in a certain situation. The same goes for the bowlers or fielders. This kind of modeling is especially critical in the case of a T20 game, where one ball or over makes the difference between losing and winning.

The fact is, like in the case of baseball, the traits that we have talked about cricketers may be inherent ones. They can be honed and improved, but not made to learn. You are either a good runner or a good fielder, or you are not. You can either perform under pressure, or you cannot.

So, a highly improved statistical model in cricket can enable us to value the players in a more pinpointed fashion. We are sure that Badale and his team didn't have access to such information, especially in the case of the younger players they purchased. Only because such information about each and every first-class game or college match hasn't been recorded, or analyzed.

Therefore, we are sure that there is no way that Rajasthan Royals could have replicated the Oakland A's model. It is only in retrospect that Badale can talk about how he borrowed from Billy Beane. Going by evidence, Billy was way ahead of Badale.

However, we can admit that Badale may have tried to follow Billy's footsteps. Maybe, these are the first steps in the direction where statistics will become as important in cricket, as it has in baseball. Maybe, the time has come for all teams – at whatever levels – to focus more on statistics than what they have seen on the field. Players' performances in a few matches can be a fluke. But statistics over a period of time cannot – and don't – lie.

There was, however, one aspect that Rajasthan Royals got right, when compared to Oakland A's baseball or Portland basketball teams. In fact, the team managed to incorporate the best of both the worlds as far as captaincy or coaching was concerned.

In most cases, when teams are decided on the basis of statistics and actual performances (not perceived ones), the system in which it plays becomes absolutely critical.

According to David Halberstam, 'Portland team members saw Ramsay (the coach) as a man who believed more strongly in his system than in his players, and thus perhaps more in the coach than his material. The system came first. If you stayed within the system and ran the plays right, you won. Ramsay was stubborn about making changes, according to his players.

'... Among players Ramsay was the ultimate coach's coach, a man of consummate discipline who believed above all in his system, and seemed to have more confidence in it, the players sometimes believed, than he did in them. Everything about him was professional. Nothing was left to chance. His scouting and his breakdowns of opponents before a game were acute, complete and prophetic. He expected certain things to happen on the court and they almost always did. In his world the coach was important, very important.' This is how a statistically-driven team functions.

But then there is the other spectrum, where coaches behave differently. As Halberstam commented: 'By contrast, Wilkens (an opponent of Ramsay in the league) was known in the league as a player's coach, a coach who used certain plays but was willing to let his players follow their natural instincts, make their own adjustments on the court. Some of his players believed that he had more trust in them and their natural ability than did coaches like (Portland's) Ramsay.'

Fortunately for the Rajasthan Royals, its team combined the best of both the worlds. In their promoters, like Badale, they found someone who believed in a system, in statistics, in selecting a team where if the players performed according to their given abilities and records, i.e. according to a perceived system, a win was guaranteed. In Warne, as the captain-coach, the Royals found the other extreme: a coach, who was willing to trust his players, encourage them, and goad them to follow their instincts.

In comparison, some of the other teams in IPL got bogged down by their own strategies.

To begin with, their selection process was biased and subjective. Although Jaipur's was not as objective, or statistically driven as Badale claims, it was still driven by professional reasons. In the case of most of the other teams, the 'icon' player or the captain had a huge say in selecting his team members. As Mallya admitted, the Bangalore Royal Challengers team was entirely based on its captain, Dravid's wish list. The same thing happened with other teams like Mumbai Indians.

Mumbai Indians' captain, Tendulkar insisted on the players that he wanted in his side. This was true even for the known Indian names and the young local players. Take the examples of Ashish Nehra, India's former opening bowler, who has now moved to Delhi in the second season, and Abhishek Nayar, the twenty-year-old right-arm medium-pacer.

Prior to the first IPL season, Nehra was in the doghouse as far as national and international cricket was concerned. Plagued by a string of injuries, he hadn't bowled a ball in competitive cricket for nearly eighteen months. Most of the cricket fans had forgotten him and observers felt he had a slim chance to return to the Indian national side in the near future. Therefore, Nehra knew that IPL provided an ideal opportunity for him to return to serious cricket. It could be his comeback league.

It didn't really matter to Nehra which team he played for in IPL, but many thought that being from Delhi, he would choose Delhi Daredevils. Instead, Nehra opted for Mumbai Indians. The reason: Tendulkar told him categorically that he was welcome to turn out for his side.

This was an offer that Nehra couldn't refuse since Tendulkar had been his friend and mentor since his early cricketing days. India's best batsman had seen the fast bowler right from his formative years, and was open in admiration for Nehra's swing at high speeds. (Nehra's best moment came during the 2007 World Cup, when he became the fastest Indian bowler with a ball that clocked 149.5 kmph on the speed gun during India's match against Zimbabwe.)

Since Tendulkar couldn't play the first few matches because of an injury and, Mumbai Indians lost the services of off-spinner Harbhajan Singh after the controversial 'slapgate' incident, Nehra played in all the fourteen matches during the IPL. 'The most important thing for me was to play in as many matches as possible. I didn't set any match performances' targets,' he admitted.

Although Mumbai Indians' fortunes failed in IPL, Nehra did come across as a winner. In fact, he practically remembered every ball that he bowled in the tournament. 'My economy rate was fairly good for someone who bowled during power play, and during the death overs. I was also perhaps the only Indian bowler to win a man of the match award in the first half of the first IPL season.'

He added that 'I felt in good rhythm. I only have to play a few four-days matches and bowl long spells to get my fitness back to the best. Getting my pace and swing back is just a matter of time.'

Similarly, Abhishek Nayar was another player handpicked by Tendulkar to be part of Mumbai Indians. Tendulkar had been Nayar's hero since his childhood, and Nayar had the pleasure to play with the master batsman during the 2005 Ranji Trophy season. However, before the IPL, Nayar wasn't sure if Tendulkar would remember him.

'Remember, he did, and the first words he told me during the pre-IPL camp were: "Whatever you do, do it naturally. Don't get bothered by me, or any other big guys around you."' Nayar too got an extended run in IPL due to injuries and the ban that plagued the Mumbai Indians team.

According to several players and other people attached with the Bangalore team, Dravid was intensely involved in the selection process. Later, his critics complained that since he is a great test batsman, he picked up players, who should have been a part of a Test XI and not a T20 team. More importantly, captains like Dravid took themselves, and their cricket, too seriously.

Most of the younger players in the Bangalore team viewed that as a compliment and as a matter of respect for their captain. One of them, Bharat Chipli, said that it was fascinating to see that players like Dravid, who have been playing cricket for decades, and had scored over 20,000 runs in first class cricket, 'still wanted to work and improve his batting technique. He was basically into his game; he batted for nearly two hours at the nets even after achieving so much.'

However, the flip side of this was that Dravid never managed to loosen his team members like Warne did. He never could get his players to enjoy the game. As Chipli puts it without being critical of his captain: 'Dravid remained silent most of the times. He didn't talk too much, and only replied if he was directly approached by a player. He was very focused about cricket; he talked little even at the nets.' Another player commented that only cricket was discussed at the nets and during practice games.

Therefore, there was this underlying pressure to perform or to do as well as Dravid had in the past. None of the players, especially the younger ones, felt light. This was exactly the opposite of what happened with Rajasthan Royals, where the players had fun and, hence, were desperate to deliver their best, only to please a captain they respected.

In retrospect, Chipli said that the opening pair is critical in T20. It has to score runs fast, and not lose wickets. 'In T20 games, self-confidence is the most important issue, not your technique. But we didn't get off to a good start in most games. As an opener, I played three matches and my highest was ten. This was one reason why we didn't do well. However, my confidence has gone up after IPL.'

The lack of self-confidence was evident in the Hyderabad team too, as was admitted by almost everyone connected with the team – younger players, administrators and coaches. Kanwaljeet Singh, Deccan Chargers' assistant coach in the first season candidly admitted that there was too much of pre-match planning that happened in the dressing room and on the nets.

'In T20, pre-match planning doesn't work most of the times. A captain and coach have to be extremely flexible. The former has to take almost-instant decisions on the field depending on the match and the requirements at that particular moment. Things change in a 20-over game very quickly. So, the captain has to be well prepared for all kinds of eventualities. The mind has to work constantly and consistently. One never knows how the complexion of the game can change in a couple of balls and overall strategies need to be changed right there and then.

'The captain has to be sharp enough to effect those changes on the field; the strategic adjustments have to be instant. There can be no set pre-match plan for a 20-over game. One can start with such a plan, but have to change it based on situations. This is especially true about bowling, where bowlers need to have the ability to adjust almost after every few balls.'

One of the younger players, who interacted with the first season's coach Robin Singh, former national cricketer, accepted that the coach came up with a plan before the match. 'But there were no changes in the plan during the match. In fact, if we won the game, he would proudly claim that it was because everyone had followed his pre-match instructions and stuck to the plan. When we lost, he blamed us, pointing out the particular balls or overs, where we didn't stick to his plan, or the strokes we played. It was always our fault if we lost the match, and his credit if we won it.'

Another player gave the example of one particular match, where Rajasthan Royals executed an exciting last-over win over Deccan Chargers. This was the match when Warne cracked 17 runs in Symonds' last over, and many blamed Hyderabad's captain VVS Laxman for it.

'I felt happy during the game as I had bowled well and had even taken a wicket. So, when the game entered the death over, I thought I would be asked to bowl the last over of the match. I was shocked when captain Laxman tossed the ball to Symonds. As you know, we lost the game. Later, everyone I knew came up to me and said that they were convinced that we would win the match as I would definitely bowl the last over. I felt proud that people had the same confidence in me that I had, but also felt sad at the same time that we lost a match that we could have won.'

V Mohan Raj, who was the manager of the Hyderabad team in the first season agreed and added that even in the pre-match planning, there was total confusion and chaos. It was as if there was no strategy at all – either pre-match or during the matches.

'The batting order was all wrong; we sent the wrong person at the wrong time. In T20, you need to send your best strikers first – the best at No. 1, and the next best at No. 2. We had specialist openers and strikers, and sending them in the right order should have been a priority. So, while Gilchrist was the best opener, we had problems with the second opener. We kept changing Gilchrist's partner, and this was the cause of instability in our batting. We didn't have the best five strikers going in, in the same order. We should have done it irrespective of the results. It would have been a huge confidence-booster for all the players. T20 is about choosing the best five batsmen and the best five bowlers; there is no need to experiment with six batsmen and four bowlers, or any other combination.

'For instance, none of the bowlers knew or realized who really was the strike bowler in the team. There were many instances, when the top bowlers either didn't bowl a single over, or didn't finish their requisite quota. In three or four games, fast bowler RP Singh didn't finish his quota of four overs. In many matches, spinner Pragyan Ojha didn't get to bowl at all. This showed a lack of planning in the field. In contrast, Warne was the one man who ran the ship; he was in total control and he was thinking on his feet.

'For many cricketers, coaches and administrators, T20 was a new concept, and they didn't know what to do. Teams that did better in the first season were ones that experimented with their strategies, especially on the field. They took decisions regardless of being right or wrong. Taking decisions regularly, changing your tactics regularly is critical in T20.

'The end result (for the Hyderabad team) was chaos; no player knew what role he had to actually play. The message was either not communicated or understood properly. The same kind of mistakes were repeated match after match. We lost some seven games in the last over. We should have at least won two out of them without any problems. All these close games could have gone either way. This tells a definitive story of what was wrong with the Deccan Chargers. Our team didn't have a dynamic approach.'

Another problem with Deccan Chargers was that there was no collective effort to formulate strategies, or to seek other's advice when the current ones were going wrong.

Mohan Raj, who has played first class cricket and claimed to have considerable knowledge about the game, was clearly pissed off.

'We were made to sit out and watch the matches. We were never given any opportunities to pass comments to the think tank (which consisted mainly of three people), or to give advice to plug any gaps in the existing strategies. It could have been a good idea to allow a manager, who had knowledge about the game and who observed the performances during all the matches, to give critical inputs. It could have been a positive development. But it didn't happen. No one asked us anything, and we were clearly told not to get involved with the game. Even the franchisee asked us to stay away. We spoke to the franchisee, but their confidence on the team's think tank was very high. I don't blame the franchise owner, but I am sure that in the next season, the franchisees will become smarter.'

Many of those who were closely connected with the Hyderabad team also blamed the senior players for the lack of team's performance. Mohan Raj believed that there was no communication either between all the senior players, or between the seniors and the juniors. 'The coach, captain and Gilchrist were not able to completely share their strategies with the rest of the team.'

He added that the 'desire to win in any team has to be a collective one. It happens only when all the players have something to look forward to. In the case of many senior players in the Deccan Chargers team, they thought that they had already achieved a lot in the international scene. So, there was no desire to perform in IPL. Hence, there was no cohesion within the team, and there was no sharing of ownership each time the team won or lost.'

Kanwaljeet Singh shared the same logic, although he supported his captain and the team. 'The stars in our team were under no pressure to perform, and they were quite relaxed about IPL. Except for a couple of players, none of the seniors performed. For example, our bowling became the weak link as it didn't click at all. We had good international bowlers, but they failed to deliver the goods. Sri Lankan veteran Chaminda Vaas was off colour. RP Singh wasn't consistent throughout the tournament. Scott Styris, the New Zealander, also didn't perform.

'Even among the batsmen, Herschelle Gibbs didn't perform. The team was not short of capability or experience, but we didn't show it on the field. It came as a complete shock to us that some of the best international players didn't work out for us. We just didn't click as a team. For example, if we had won the initial three close games, the momentum could have been different. We could have taken off from there.'

In fact, Singh went a step further to trash the current contract system in IPL. 'I think there shouldn't be a three-year contract for the players. A franchise owner should be able to change players every year in case they didn't perform as per the expectations. A three-year contract meant that the players would continue to earn huge sums whether they played well or not. Hence, the attitude of some of the players wasn't right. But players cannot play around with other people's money. The franchisee was doing its best, but the players' minds have to be good for the team to win. T20 is all about smarter and sharper players. It is all about the survival of the fittest or the best. One cannot hide the (non-performing) players. A team will be exposed if its players are either not good or performing as per their potential.'

According to Singh, the local and younger players were more interested in giving off their best. 'It should have been the opposite, but it wasn't.' In addition, the younger lads were keen to learn to be able to adjust their game to the T20 format.

For instance, Ojha bowled well as he changed his bowling tactics after listening to the assistant coach. 'I was given the task of looking at the bowling of the local players. I asked Ojha to adjust his line and length, to bowl at the stumps. I also urged him to lower his trajectory so that he could push the ball faster through the air, and use the width of the crease, so that he could make subtle variations to confuse batsmen. In T20, one cannot be stereotyped. There have to be constant variations, even if subtle, in line, length and angle.'

One more example from Deccan Chargers should be enough to show the conflict between players of different statures, the chasm between the coach and players, and also the chaos that prevailed within the team.

According to a younger member of the Deccan Chargers: 'Most times the coach couldn't handle the foreign or senior players. He couldn't say anything to them if they did something wrong on the field, or took wrong decisions. So, he took out his anger and frustration on the local and younger players. Each time we lost a match, or some senior goofed up, the coach would either call us before the next game, or after a loss, for an intensive fielding practice for 2-3 hours. Sometimes, we would finish at 6 p.m., just an hour or so before the next match would begin. In the same vein, most of the foreign players would never come for training. Only Gilchrist did; all the others sat in the dressing room.

'I thought that the coach should be professional, but Robin couldn't do it. In addition, I felt that the coach and captain should choose a proper XI and let them play. But our coach restricted our play and natural instincts. And the young players didn't have the guts to reply back or say anything on his face. Before IPL, I thought a coach was never that important in cricket. Now, I feel he is the most important member.'

Fortunately, in the case of Warne and Rajasthan Royals, none of these issues existed. Warne was the coach and captain; in fact, he was the one-man think tank of the team, who asked for suggestions from others like Smith. Rajasthan Royals had no seniors or international stars to contend with; all of them, except Smith, were too junior or young to question Warne. All of them would do exactly what they were told to, and even die to do what their captain asked them to do. There were no questions about practice or nets, as Warne himself wasn't too strict about them. So, when they were held, everyone attended since it was not mandatory or forced upon them.

In a sense, there were neither conflicts nor chaos. There was total clarity since only one person was thinking about the matches, and changing strategies and tactics after every ball, or after each over. Change was a constant with Warne.

As almost everyone in the Jaipur team wanted to do well and succeed, the captain didn't have to urge them to do so. Rajasthan Royals had nothing to lose. If it did well, it would get the praises; if it did badly, no one would notice as the team was written off right at the beginning of the league. So, each player desperately wanted to do well – for himself, his team and for Warne.

To help the team gel together, Warne went to great lengths. For one, he learnt Hindi so that he could communicate with some of the players. He went beyond the customary *Namaste*. In one of the matches, he was even heard speaking an entire sentence in Hindi, as if it was his second language. To create an atmosphere where everyone would be comfortable with him and with each other, he gave nicknames to all the players instilling a sense of informality and friendliness.

However, unlike what Badale maintained, there wasn't any grand strategy in choosing the players, captain, or in finding inefficiencies in the market to select the best players at the lowest possible price. Rajasthan Royals' win was more by chance than stats or strategy.

From Gully Passions to 'Gilly' Religion

There were several non-cricketing issues that IPL raised. What will happen to the youngsters, who got the chance of their lives and gained instant fame? Like the many cricketers we had seen while playing for a renowned club in Delhi and as avid observers, we were compelled to think whether they too will hang out with unbuttoned shirts, collars up, chains dangling round their necks and girls hovering around them? Does the same happen to cricketers from other nations? Does Andrew Symonds or Adam Gilchrist (Gilly) behave like self-proclaimed celebrities? Do they become like Yuvraj Singh, Ravi Shastri, Murli Karthik and Vinod Kambli?

We got some answers as we walked into Bangalore's RCI Grounds to meet Devraj Patil, the youngster who had played for Royal Challengers. In the morning, Devraj had asked us to meet him during lunchtime as he was playing a club match; he added that he was unlikely to be in the middle as his team was batting, the openers were still at the wicket, and he was to go in at No. 4. So, we asked one of his teammates about Patil's whereabouts.

'He's in the middle,' came the reply.

'But how come he's batting? Have you already lost two wickets?'

'No. But now that he has played IPL, he decided to go in early.'

We could sense a huge mass of envy hanging in the air as other teammates teetered at the reply. Our impression got strengthened when we heard laughter as Devraj got out cheaply without reaching double figures. There was tension in the air, and it had nothing to do with the game that was being played. As we had expected, bad vibes and feelings were running high as other younger players felt that they should have got the chance to play IPL, rather than the ones who were selected.

There was uneasiness and a feeling that politics had again won the day in Indian cricket.

The moment we met Bharat Chipli, who was lounging on the balcony after having got out for 96 and was another young cricketer who represented the Royal Challengers in IPL, we asked him a direct question. 'Do your mates treat you differently after IPL? And have you changed as a person and cricketer in the past few months?'

'No, I haven't changed. I am still the same person. I don't make extra requests when I talk to my colleagues in the club team. We still talk to each other; we still scold each other if someone has played stupidly or badly. What you heard must have been a joke or a few people having fun. Only the players who are younger to me (in age or in the team) show more respect than they did earlier.'

Later, as we talked about other things, we noticed that this twenty-five year old's eyes were constantly on the game. He watched each shot and ball, appreciated it, and made comments on the match's progress. 'Good shot, nice drive, well bowled. The two pacers have suddenly started swinging the ball, they are bowling really well. I missed my century due to a lapse in concentration. I went to drive an outswinger. Just like that,' he said as Devraj was beaten by a beauty of an outswinger that pitched on the off stump.

The only aberration to his seriousness about cricket was his half-buttoned white shirt, his slight swagger as he walked away, and the gold chain around his neck.

Among the South-based young IPL-returned cricketers we met, there wasn't any sense of arrogance or non-cricketing airs about them. They all seemed serious and devoted sportsmen who saw IPL as an opportunity to do bigger, better things in their careers. Many of them weren't even thinking of the next IPL season; they were more interested in the next club game, the coming Ranji season, and figuring out ways to further improve their performance. The chapter about the first IPL season was closed as far as they were concerned. For them, IPL was just one more stepping stone on their cricketing path.

An unassuming medium pacer, Sarvesh Kumar was another young player who got an opportunity to play for Hyderabad's Deccan Chargers. For him, 'IPL is only the beginning. Now, I have fixed targets for the next three to four years. I have to perform well in the next IPL season. I have to give my best. I did reasonably well in the first season (bowled three overs for 18 runs against the Delhi Daredevils and gave away similar runs in two overs in the next match), but I have to do better. My performance in Ranji Trophy has to be consistent, and I hope to play for the country within the next four years.' As a parting shot, with a cute mischievous smile, he added, 'Earlier no one knew who Sarvesh Kumar was, now people recognize me on the street.'

We went back home with a nice feeling in our hearts. Players like Chipli, Devraj and Sarvesh proved that the future of Indian cricket was in secure hands. These budding cricketers were likely to become sober sportsmen like Tendulkar, Dravid, Javagal Srinath and Anil Kumble, rather than truants such as Harbhajan, Zaheer, Yuvraj, and Ganguly.

Even as we write this, we remember the story of Virat Kohli, the Delhi-based youngster who played in IPL. The day after his father died, Virat showed up for a Ranji game for his state, and scored a brilliant, almost chanceless, and a match-winning knock. For these players cricket was more than a religion. It was their Yin and Yang, God and Goddess, spiritual guru and philosopher.

UGLY AUSTRALIANS

Invariably, great sportsmen are great characters. Skill and talent is vital. Hard work is critical. Seizing opportunities is crucial. But more than that, it's the attitude and the manner in which they treat the game that makes them what they become. This is even true of the Aussie cricketers, who many Indian fans feel are 'low life'.

Over the years, like was the case with the 'Ugly American' image during the Vietnam war, the Australian cricketers gained a reputation of being brash, brazen, arrogant, in-your-face, and unsportsmanlike-like. They lacked a sense of fair play. For them, winning at any cost was all-important. Nothing else mattered. This seemed truer after India's tour of Australia, just before IPL's first season. The Harbhajan-Monkey affair and the manner in which the Aussies won the Sydney test by claiming false catches gave finality to such impressions about Australian players like Ricky Ponting and Andrew Symonds.

'All the stories that you read and heard about Symonds during the India-Australia test series are bullshit and crap. There is no truth in them,' averred the hurly-burly Sikh, Kanwaljeet Singh, who was the assistant coach for Deccan Chargers. (Australians like Symonds and Gilchrist played for the Chargers.) According to him, Symonds is the best team player that he has ever seen, either as a cricketer, observer or coach.

'Symonds is a fantastic human being. He is a complete team player. If the captain wanted him to bowl, he would do that. If the skipper wanted him to bat at any other position, not his normal one, he would gladly do it. At crunch moments, he would deliver even while fielding by taking that fantastic catch or stopping a sure four. Some players walked away when asked to give that extra bit, but not Symonds. Totally committed to his game he treated the Chargers as his own team. He, along with Gilly (Adam Gilchrist), was friendly with all the boys, including the junior ones.'

That's the reason why all the younger players in the Hyderabad team adored Gilly and Symonds. Always ready with a word of advice or encouragement they would come down to the youngsters' level, instead of behaving like stars and celebrities. They were cricketers, just like Sarvesh and Kalyan Krishna (another youngster in the Deccan Chargers team) were. There was no difference between them as Sarvesh and Kalyan had the potential to become the next Gilly and Symonds.

For Sarvesh and Kalyan, playing with Gilly was like a dream come true. 'When I played the first IPL match, and I ran in to bowl my first ball, I couldn't imagine that Gilly was keeping wickets to me. I was really excited,' revealed Kalyan. Sarvesh was surprised how Gilly gave 100 per cent at the nets and in the games, even if he was not 100 per cent fit. 'He was a great motivator at the nets, in the field and during team meetings. Even if someone misfielded, he would never scold the player. He would just say "good show".'

It was because of Gilly that Sarvesh played his first IPL match against the Delhi Daredevils. 'He realized that there was something special in me when he saw that I made efforts at the nets. Just before that match, he walked up to me and said I was playing in the game. But I wasn't completely fit and couldn't perform as well as I wanted to. But before heading back home after the tournament, he came over to me and said that I would be a different bowler in the next season.'

However, more than being excellent cricketers, these international players turned out to be amazing human beings. They won the hearts of their younger teammates. Kalyan reminisced how Gilly came and sat with him on one of the numerous flights that the Hyderabad team took to play the IPL matches. 'We were coming back from Delhi when he asked me about my family. I told him about the recent death of my dad. He felt sorry. He said, "Kaddu, that's how he called me, take care of your family." He and Symonds were legends for us.

'Before the tournament, I had read somewhere that Gilchrist was the richest cricketer. But he was so simple; he would stay in any room without complaining during our trips. Several times, he would sit with me for food. After IPL, when I went to the

MRF Foundation camp, he would call me several times from Australia and inquire about my game and also about other younger players like Venu Gopal and Pragyan Ojha. He even asked me how he should address me.'

No wonder, Sarvesh too became a complete Gilly fan. 'During our practice matches, I ensured that I was always in his team. On a given day, if he wore a yellow T-shirt, I wore yellow. If he wore green, I wore green too. Life *mein Gilly ke jaisa rehna chahiye* [In life, one should be like Gilly].'

Though there was one problem that Sarvesh had with Gilly. He didn't know how to address him. 'Everyone called him Gilly or Gilchrist. But I was confused, how could I call such a senior player Gilly? But I found a way out by calling him Brother.'

It was evident to anyone and everyone that players like Gilly and Symonds enjoyed the game and their lives as cricketers.

The last word on Symonds came from assistant coach Kanwaljeet Singh. 'Despite our numerous defeats in IPL, he never allowed team members to feel demoralized. He always did things to boost up their spirits. He would crack jokes, imitate people, especially, the team's trainer. During one of the flights, when we were returning after losing to Mumbai Indians, Symonds removed the newspapers from the seats of every team member. When asked why he did it, he replied that he didn't want anyone to sulk after reading the news about how they had lost the match.'

Another incident Kanwaljeet can never forget is his birthday in 2008 that he celebrated with the Deccan Chargers. 'Along with other team members, Gilly and Symonds came for the party. They were shocked and surprised when people smeared the birthday cake all over my face. They thought that it was an Indian tradition of sorts. So, when Gilly celebrated his marriage anniversary, both asked why no one was doing the same to them. In fact, they urged people to rub the cake on their faces.'

Even in other IPL teams, international players became a hit with the younger, not-so-known local players. Mark Boucher and Jacques Kallis helped Chipli with his game. 'They taught us about the drills and practice methods they use to hone their skills. They taught me how to improve body movement, which was really helpful especially for an opener like me. They would hit a tennis ball with a racket at high speed towards me and I had to move as if I was batting against a pace bowler. They told me about the exercises they did regularly. I learned so much from seeing them bat at the nets and in the matches.'

Palani Amarnath, a young medium pace bowler in the Chennai team, was ecstatic that he was in the squad that was led by India's captain, Dhoni, and included many of his childhood heroes such as Mathew Hayden and Muralidaran. 'Like all Indian kids, I dreamt of getting their autographs one day. I just didn't know what to do when I met them for the first time as teammates.'

His life was made a bit easy, as was the case with many other younger players in IPL, when the internationally acclaimed players simply walked up to their unfancied (and amateur) colleagues, introduced themselves and made the latter feel at ease. 'We had great team spirit. All the seniors were always cracking jokes and were ready to help us. I had a long bowling session with Jacob Oram (of New Zealand) and he made me better my slower delivery and the bouncer. Makhaya Ntini (of South Africa) had a great sense of humour. I don't think he knows what it is to be sad and serious. He would try hard to sing Bollywood and Tamil movie songs and do funny imitation of other team members. On the field, he would encourage local bowlers to try different variations such as bowling wide off the crease or with a shorter run-up.'

QUITE UNLIKE CRICKET

Years ago, when he was in school, the now twenty-year-old Sarvesh Kumar thought he was like thousands of other children from lower and middle-class families. Like most conservative families, his parents wanted him to study hard, get a professional degree, find a plum job, and forget about cricket. Petty politics, not-too-much money unless one joined the select few who played for their country, and the absence of a benevolent benefactor convinced such parents that there was no future for their kids as cricketers.

This was especially true in the case of Sarvesh, whose father is a welder in the government-owned ordnance factory in Hyderabad, and still travels the 60 km distance from the neighbouring town of Medak every working day to commute to office using the inter-city bus service. For years, the family has faced financial troubles of some sort or the other. As Sarvesh reminisced: '*Ghar pe bahut* financial problems *the* [There were many financial problems at home].' In addition, Sarvesh as the only son – sandwiched between two sisters – was the only potential bread winner, who could help tide over these issues but only if he abandoned cricket, and took up a 'decent' job.

'Although my dad did support my passion for cricket, he was apprehensive about my future.' What's there in cricket? Why don't you take up a regular job? were the questions that he would ask Sarvesh often. In 2006, he also had a major showdown with his father over the same issue. The situation came to a head when, after the end of the year's cricket season in November 2006, Sarvesh decided to call it quits. Circumstances made him believe his life would be better off listening to his father. Thank God he finally didn't.

Thank God for Rajendra Reddy, who saved Sarvesh's cricketing career.

'The credit for my career in sports goes to Rajendra Reddy, my first coach, who encouraged and supported me in all respects. Convinced that I had a future in this game he helped me change my decision. I continued to play cricket because of his cricketing, moral, emotional, philosophical, and even financial support,' said the lean and lanky Sarvesh in an interview at Hyderabad's Gymkhana Grounds, where he practices every evening. And without telling his dad, Sarvesh played the Hyderabad league in the 2007 season.

Fortunately for him, he found yet another angel patron in Maheshwar Singh. Coach of the combined districts team, Maheshwar Singh felt that it was cruel for Sarvesh to be making constant trips from Medak to Hyderabad and back to play serious cricket. 'Sir said please don't do this. It will affect your concentration. He asked me to stay at his house in Hyderabad, and for eight months, the former Ranji Trophy batsman took care of me in this city. I played in Hyderabad because of his generous backup.'

In early 2008, IPL happened for Sarvesh. And his personal and professional (cricketing) life changed dramatically.

Sometime in March 2008, this young, unassuming and boyish-looking youngster got an unexpected call from Kanwaljeet Singh. 'He called me and said that I was playing in IPL for the Hyderabad team. I thanked him, and then walked into an empty, silent room in the house. It took some time for the news to sink in. Then I was "full happy". I immediately called up my dad and all the close relatives and friends. No one had thought this could happen to me. My relatives knew that I played cricket, but they never knew that I played at a serious level and could achieve this. During the IPL, all of them came to see the matches and the known national and international players in action.'

As we sat on a chipped and cracked wooden table outside the equally dilapidated canteen at the Gymkhana Grounds, Sarvesh, in a mix of Hindi, Telugu and English, remembered the offer in greater details. 'Based on my performance, it was not entirely unexpected. I have been playing for Medak district for years, participated in the prestigious Moin-ud-Ullah cricket tournament in Andhra Pradesh for two years, represented the state U-19 (with 19 wickets in 2008), U-22 and U-25 teams.

'I was even selected for the one-dayers, where I got a five-wicket haul in the first match, and took eleven wickets in five matches. More importantly, I played Deodhar Trophy without having been selected for the state Ranji Trophy team, which played four-day matches. No one in the state had ever played Deodhar Trophy without getting into the Ranji side first. But IPL was still unexpected and came out of the blue.'

Similar are the stories of several other young and talented domestic players, who did harbour the dream to play in the much-hyped IPL tournament because of their recent performances. But they were sure that it wouldn't happen as they were relatively unknown players, except in the local cricketing circles. Talented yes, but they were not networked with the powerful circles. They had the skill, but no one to push their cases with key selectors.

But somewhere, deep down, they knew that they were living in an age of opportunities. They realized that this was the time when meritocracy had a much better chance to triumph than ever before. In post-reforms India, as red tape was slashed, bureaucracy banished from several areas, licence-quota regime liberalized, the burgeoning middle class moved on to centre stage. It led to an ongoing clash between tradition and modernity, morals and materialism, the older generation and GenR(eformed).

This also resulted in a silent revolution in Indian sports. For decades, in millions of lower- and middle-class homes, the sons and daughters had lost a key battle with their parents. The children invariably gave in to their parents' belief that education was more important than sports, which was riddled with politics and money power. Respectability in society, said the parents, came from becoming an engineer, a doctor, or an IAS officer. Most youngsters buckled under such pressures.

However, things changed in the 1990s. As India became a software power, young Indians became ambitious. Conquering foreign territories, the new generation was growing confident. As the country was taken seriously globally, teenagers became convinced that their time had come. As Manmohan Singh, India's former finance minister said in his first budget speech in 1991 – India was the idea whose time had come.

In cricket, the catalysts turned out to be corporatization, eyeball culture, and India's stature in international cricket. Budding sportsmen like Sarvesh Kumar decided to take their destiny in their own hands. Confident of the changing times they decided to grab whatever opportunities came their way – against their parents' wishes unlike what children had done in the past. They dreamt, they fought, and they conquered.

Since his school days, Chipli wanted to become a cricketer. This kid from Bangalore took commerce in college so that he could devote more time to his game. Obviously, his dad, who wanted him to pursue his studies in science, vehemently opposed this. (Science as a subject was always more valued than commerce.) 'The only reason my dad allowed me to play cricket was because I ensured that I did well in studies, and this kept him happy. And when I became a professional by becoming a part of the Karnataka Ranji team, and got a job with Canara Bank on sports quota, he was satisfied,' explained Chipli, while we sat on the balcony of Bangalore's RCI Grounds watching a game.

After representing Karnataka in the U-19, 22, and 25 teams, and playing Ranji Trophy for his state for three years with eight centuries, Chipli got his first big break. He got a call from none other than Rahul Dravid.

'Dravid told me that I would be a part of the Bangalore IPL team. I was thrilled that finally I had a chance at the highest level to prove my mettle. My family too was happy, but not overjoyed. Dad didn't show any reaction at all. However, I knew I had a chance to make it to the Bangalore team. During the auction, when teams purchased international and national players, bowlers were the most sought after. So, I realized that Bangalore needed batsmen, and that I had fair odds on my side.'

Since the beginning, the odds were stacked against Devraj Patil, Chipli's teammate in the Karnataka and Bangalore IPL teams. After getting out cheaply, Devraj joined me on the balcony of the RCI Grounds. Carrying a lunch box with a masala dosa that was given free by the club and, later, barking an order for curd rice, he narrated how he became an IPL star.

'I am from Shimoga (a tourist destination) and my family still stays there. I stay in Bangalore to be able to play cricket, and I work at the Central Board for Excise and Customs, a job I got under sports quota. It was when I was in the ninth standard that I shifted to Bangalore. There was a friend of mine, and we used to play together in Shimoga. Then he moved to Bangalore. During one of his annual school vacation visit to Shimoga, he asked me to come to Bangalore. He convinced me that my cricketing future lay in the shift to the state capital. I moved to Bangalore and stayed with my uncle who supported me completely.'

Obviously, Devraj's family was upset, to say the least. His parents were not interested in cricket and, for them, it must have been sacrilege for the son to take the decision on several counts. One, he was leaving home, not for studies or better job prospects, but for a game they didn't understand. Two, he was taking the decision under the influence of a friend, and conservative parents think that friends are bad influences for their children. Finally, the son's future seemed uncertain.

But Devraj persisted. From his uncle's home, he was able to move into a hostel. 'The hostel was free for me because I was a cricketer. But my uncle paid for whatever expenses I incurred and encouraged me.'

Like Chipli and other younger players in IPL, Devraj played for his state in the U-16, 19, 22, and 25 teams. He made his Ranji debut in 2007, and played two games scoring a total of 13 runs. However, his real claim to fame came during the domestic T20 tournament where, playing for Karnataka, he was the state's highest scorer with just over 200 runs in nine matches. In fact, he enjoyed a century partnership with Dravid in the game against Orissa. 'So, Rahul (Dravid) knew how I played,' he told us with a wry smile.

Still, Devraj was taken by surprise when he got that all-important call from Dravid. 'I couldn't imagine my luck. I was at home; I ate lunch and watched television allowing the news to sink in. But my family never watched cricket or the IPL matches. My dad, who never approved of my interest in cricket, was okay with it only after I got a job.' Devraj's dad, in many ways, didn't care about cricket, or IPL and its implications.

Even in those rare cases, where the dad did take an active interest in his son's cricket, there were other issues to deal with. One of them always happened to be household finances. Kalyan Krishna's is one such story.

A young boy from Vijaywada in Andhra Pradesh, Kalyan played in school and college, and now has six Ranji, three Deodhar and two Duleep Trophy seasons behind him. For the Andhra Pradesh's Ranji team, this fast bowler, who shares the new ball with colleague Vijay Kumar (who also played in IPL), has taken 140 wickets in less than 40 innings. Over the years, he has been guided by coaches like Bose Babu (his first) and Nirmal Kumar (his current mentor), and administrators like Chamundi Sinha (secretary of the state cricket board). Like many Indian players, he has played in the English minor county league.

'My dad loved that I played cricket. This was despite one of my relatives, who played for Vijaywada, always saying that there was too much of politics and money involved in cricket. I too thought that I should focus on studies, but I stuck to cricket only because of my father. He maintained that I should play well, and should not care about politics.

'However, my dad is not working for the past few years now. He was a real estate consultant, took some bad decisions, incurred huge losses, and the family was burdened with heavy debt. We were in a bad shape financially.'

Being selected in the Hyderabad IPL team turned out to be god-sent for Kalyan. 'Chamundi sir called up the manager for the Ranji Trophy one-day team, who informed me about the selection. I couldn't believe it. Professionally, I thought I had no chance. I felt that Deccan Chargers, being a Hyderabad team would consider players from the same city, and not from the rest of the state. But it selected players from three different regions. I am thankful, or else I would have stood no chance. IPL helped me take care of my family; it helped me repay all our debts. With the remaining money, I plan to buy some land or plots.'

The beauty of IPL – and the changed environment in Indian sports – was that it gave opportunities even to those who had never dreamt of playing cricket, let alone representing the country or rubbing shoulders with international stars. One of them was Chennai's P Amarnath, who even today doesn't look like a professional cricketer. When we met him at the office of India

Cements, where he works and which is the owner of Chennai Super Kings, he was wearing a checkered light blue shirt, navy blue Peter England trousers (the team's official off-the-field apparel partner) and leather sandals. He could have passed off as one of the thousands of mid-level executives in the office.

Amarnath offered a nervous handshake and sat uncomfortably on the edge of a steel tube chair that you normally find in government offices. It was probably the first time that he was talking to a journalist, or so he looked. And he seemed pressured as we started the conversation in English; only when we switched to Tamil, his mother tongue did we see relief on his face. Armed with a diploma in civil engineering, Amarnath began working at a construction site in Vellore, a town in north Tamil Nadu, as a daily wage employee in 2004. With his widowed mother working for the state electricity board, Amarnath's meagre monthly salary of around Rs 2,500 was critical for the family's survival.

Back then, the thought of playing cricket for a living or earning huge sums from sports never crossed his mind. His cricketing excursions in those days were limited to playing tennis ball matches with friends. Things changed only when his friends, who were impressed by the speed he generated with the tennis ball, urged him to participate in the fast-bowling talent hunt roadshow, Scorpio Speedster.

That was the first time that he held the red leather cherry in his hand. During the talent hunt, he bowled consistently at around 120 kmph and finished fourth in the regional round. A chance acquaintance asked him if he was interested in playing fourth division club cricket in Chennai. This signalled the beginning of Amarnath's sports career. He started off with one of the clubs that were promoted by the Murugappa Group, a south India-based conglomerate.

Soon, he was recruited by Grand Slam, which was one of the several local teams owned by India Cements. Consistent performances in the lower leagues forced selectors to give him a chance to bowl in the nets for India Cements' first division team. This led to a chance to play in the Buchi Babu Cup, a premier pre-Ranji season tournament in south India. After several players from Tamil Nadu Ranji team were banned because they decided to play for rebel ICL, Amarnath got into the state team. The turning point in his embryonic career came during the inaugural T20 tournament at Vishakhapatnam (Andhra Pradesh), where he took the prized wicket of India's superstar, Tendulkar. 'He was beaten by pace as I bowled a near-perfect inswinger,' said Amarnath with his tongue firmly in his cheek. When Chennai Super Kings announced its IPL team, Amarnath's friends called to congratulate him on his inclusion. However, Amarnath initially thought that the calls were pranks played by his friends. He didn't believe when he saw his name in the newspapers; he felt that the name had been printed by mistake. Again he was wrong, as he was when he thought that his future lay as a civil engineer, and not as a national cricketer.

THE NEW ROAD TO SUCCESS

IPL will possibly change the concept of pride for cricketers-to-be. Until April 2008, cricketers thought that a large part of their mission ended when they wore the whites at Lords, or the 'blues' at Eden Gardens. It happened when they heard that roar as they ran in to bowl their first ball, or cracked that first boundary off the front foot. They felt that they had arrived when they were part of the national team that heard the heavy sound of silence as Javed Miandad hit the last-ball yorker for a six at Sharjah, or the screams and shrieks as Sreesanth caught Misbah-ul-Haq during the T20 World Cup finals.

Not any longer. IPL has redefined pride in all respects.

Many youngsters now aim to play the IPL tournament, and not worry too much about being part of the Indian team. So, club will overtake the country, franchisees will become more important than cricket administrators, and currency will be more sought after than country caps. Many ambitions will end at – and with – IPL.

Statistics are with the would-be-IPLites. The Indian team can only select sixteen players, or less than one from each state.

In the case of IPL, especially when the number of teams participating in the league goes up, over 150 players can hope to gain instant fame and recognition. That means most of those who can get to play for a state team, will stand a chance to play IPL. Well, even those who don't play for the state teams can get selected. In the first season, many players managed to play IPL without playing a first class game.

Most likely, more people will watch IPL, compared to tests and one-dayers. The IPLites can hope to become celebrities like television starlets and movie stars within two months. If this trend catches on, several other things will follow within years.

One of them will be that more players will play for only money, and not just national pride. For the next Sarvesh or Chipli, the moneybags behind the Deccan Chargers and Royal Challengers will be more appealing than BCCI. Many will take up cricket as a career – like is the case with football, tennis and golf – rather than as a sport. Cricket will not remain a means to get that menial job in a PSU or with the few private sector firms that have cricket teams. It will become a way to earn big bucks.

Ojha of Deccan Chargers, who earned $30,000 in the first season, may suddenly find himself being offered $200,000 in the future as trading of players is allowed, as is the case with other foreign leagues like the EPL (football) and NBA (basketball). This will imply that within a few months, Ojha will make more money than Tendulkar makes in the entire year from traditional cricket, excluding his earnings from sponsorship, advertising, merchandising, business and, of course, IPL.

Thanks to the money, middle- and lower-middle-class parents will no longer be troubled if their sons (and hopefully daughters once we have a women IPL) decided to chose cricket as a profession, and not medicine or engineering.

Teaching techniques at renowned Indian business schools may undergo a change in the near future. Instead of academicians, consultants and successful corporate managers, cricketers will be paid $2,000 for a single lecture on leadership. Team managers and coaches will talk about success-oriented strategies. The business and management of cricket will become a subject in one of the semesters. And management students across the country, and even abroad, will be more willing to read books on rags-to-riches stories about Sarvesh, rather than the Garage-to-Google ones.

If you think we are joking, the change has already begun.

Take the case of Manik Rao, Sarvesh's father, who travels in a state transport bus to his factory every day. When we called him one evening, he was waiting at the bus stand in Hyderabad to go back to his home in Medak. When we told him that we would call back later when he reached home, he said: 'It will be too late then, and I will go to sleep immediately as I have to wake up very early. Just wait ... (after a 30-40 seconds wait) Now we can talk. I have got into the bus.' He was simply excited to talk to us. He left us with no option, and we carried on a conversation in broken Telugu amidst the din and the high decibel level.

'I am satisfied ... I am very happy with all this. But he has to play more, he has to do well. It will be good if he plays for India. I saw my first match at a stadium during IPL, and watched other matches on television.'

But the real eye-opener came when we asked him whether he was happy that his son was playing cricket, instead of focusing on studies. (Remember what Sarvesh had said about his father having always questioned his decision to play cricket.)

'I did think sometimes that a boy in a family like ours has to study. But I always encouraged him to play cricket. Whenever I had the time, even if I had to go to the factory, I used to drop him off at cricket grounds for his matches. Everyone in the family contributed to his success on the field. He has worked a lot and now I am satisfied that he will easily get a job after playing in IPL.'

Other parents too have changed their mindsets. Cricket has become the new passport to success, fame, and money.

A few retired cricketers are being paid to give corporate lectures. A senior manager from an IT firm told me how he gets former players like K Srikkanth and Javagal Srinath, and commentators like Harsha Bhogle to talk on similarities between leadership qualities in sports and corporates, lessons from sports to help managers take decisions in the marketplace, and what sports can teach about corporate decision-making process.

What about the budding stars? What about the hopefuls who, until now, were only thinking of getting into the state team? We met many of them at Hyderabad's Gymkhana Grounds, and all of them seemed excited about IPL. There was a glint of hope in their eyes when they talked about the tournament. It was clear that they were eyeing being part of Deccan Chargers, Mumbai Indians, Rajasthan Royals, or Kolkata Knight Riders.

We saw it at the Gymkhana nets as a kid batsman drove a yorker over the bowler's head a.k.a Dhoni, lifted a perfect length delivery over covers like Yuvraj, and reverse swept a spinner in Tendulkar style. The pacer, whose yorker had been disdainfully dispatched, bowled a slower one from the back of his hand, a fast off-spinning delivery, and a slow bouncer as his next three balls. It was quintessential T20 cricket.

Some of the new IPL stars too feel that IPL was their road to success. Minus the T20 tournament, many of these young players could have quietly faded away, or vanished into cricketing oblivion. They would have been overshadowed by the Tendulkars and Yuvrajs, or Harbhajans and Ishants, no one outside their teams would have even recognized their names. This has happened to many players across the globe in the past.

During the late 1970s and early 1980s, a generation of West Indian fast bowlers – Van Burn Holder, Winston Davies and Norbert Philips – rued the fact that they were competing with the great quartet comprising Courtney Walsh, Curt Ambrose, and others. The former cricketers could have walked into any other team with their eyes closed, but they got minimal chances to play for the West Indian national team.

Similarly, in modern times, at least a dozen Indian batsmen can say that fate has played a similar game on them. The former Indian batting quartet (Tendulkar, Dravid, Ganguly, and Laxman) have shut the 'test' doors for many middle-order batsmen in the past decade or so. But unlike the past, for several young players, IPL is proving to be the new panacea. For them, IPL is a short cut to national and international recognition.

Consider the case of Shikhar Dhawan, who was part of the winning Delhi Ranji Trophy team and awarded the man-of-the-tournament at U-19 World Cup in 2004. He scored 400-plus runs in the 2004 U-19 tournament, and was selected for the prestigious Border-Gavaskar cricket scholarship to train at the Adelaide Academy in Australia. Despite such achievements, Shikhar's future in the national team looked too distant. In the eight-year-history of the scholarship, hardly any batsmen have made it to Team India.

It was then that Lady Luck decided to smile at Shikhar.

'Playing in IPL is almost like being in an international match. Winning the Ranji Trophy, or the award at U-19 World Cup did not give me the kind of visibility that the quick-fire IPL knocks gave me,' he felt. 'I have had good knocks in Ranji matches, and when you do that the selectors obviously take note. But the power of the matches that are telecast live and watched by millions is immense. Not only the selectors, even the fans get to know you and start talking about you.'

In an era, where buzz is as important as skills, where positive public perception and reception, and a stray commending opinion by former cricket greats or self-proclaimed television pundits can make or mar careers, IPL seems like a god-sent. Ask the brilliant Rohit Sharma, whose career took on a different, almost tangential, trajectory when former Australian captain Ian Chappell hailed him as a ready replacement for Tendulkar.

DRAVID OR YUVRAJ?

Sridhar Maturi, who handles sports-related strategies in an Indian software firm, gave us fresh insights into what the success of IPL would mean for future players. He felt that they would be a 'confused lot', as would be the case with the coaches. But why?

'National selectors already are faced with issues of who to play in which format of the game. For example, a Yusuf Pathan (brother of fast bowler Irfan Pathan) may only play T20. Laxman may get a chance only to play tests. Yuvraj will be taken in for the limited overs matches. As this trend catches on, youngsters will face the dilemma of how they should play, and how they should approach the game.'

Should they aim to become a Dravid and play in Tests? Or should they play like Dhoni with his innovative, non-cricketing shots? Should they forget about spinning the ball and concentrate on length that's critical in the shorter formats of the game? Should they forget pace and focus on slower deliveries, which are crucial in T20s?

Experts believe that the lure of IPL, with its heady mix of fame, money and instant recognition, will lead to a mass production of players, who will never have the time to settle down. It will give rise to a Manpreet Gony or an Ojha.

Both of them performed excellently in IPL. Both were selected in the Indian ODI team. They instantly became part of the Men in Blue. But their subsequent bowling spells didn't live to those IPL expectations. Maybe, it is too early to judge them. Maybe, they will do much better in the near future. Maybe Gony will become the next Venkatesh Prasad, and Ojha the next Vettori. Maybe, maybe …

The point observers make is that if IPL remains the success that it was in its first season, it will cut short the journey of many players, who will make the transition from state to national team. 'There will be no time to go through the learning curve for a Gony or an Ojha, no time to gain that experience to play at the highest level. There is a huge difference between playing for a club team, and doing the same for your country. We have seen it time and again in many other sports like football and basketball. And let's face it: Everyone is not as brilliant as Tendulkar to walk into the national team as a teenager and let his bat do all the talking over the next two decades,' says one of them.

Once money becomes the over-riding, or an important, reason to play, national pride takes a back seat – probably the 30th row from the boundary line. No player, who is in it for the moolah, can hope to emulate a Kumble, who walked in to bat with a fractured jaw, or a Richards, who scored a century batting virtually on one foot. Such stories of character, valour, tenacity and inner strength are rare in the professional circuits.

Since the IPL has only been here for less than a year, since we still don't know the real impact of the professional format of the game, it is only correct to also project the viewpoints of the league's numerous supporters. They feel that the tournament can only have a positive-positive effect on the young cricketers.

For instance, Kanwaljeet Singh believes that IPL would prove to be a much-needed booster for the youngsters. 'It has given exposure to little-known players, something we would never have seen. Today, no cricketer, if good, can be kept away from playing. It will reduce the role of politics in the entire selection process. One would never have heard of so many players without the IPL. For all you know, a player like Ojha would still have been waiting to be selected for the national team.'

In addition, he felt that the IPL format, with its set of international players, provides exposure to the younger players. It helps in uplifting both their morale and playing standards, in turn enabling them to be aware of what they will be up against when they get into the national side.

Finally, the setting of the tournament results in a different motivation for the younger players. 'Playing is one thing. But in the case of IPL, each cricketer knows that millions are watching him. Plus, he is playing with the best in the world. So, there's an urge to prove yourself. Everyone wants to do it in front of crowds and their heroes. In some ways, the crowds also charge up the players to perform better.'

On the issue of how the future generation of players is likely to become T20-oriented, the counter point is that any game requires a set of basic skills. A Dhoni can be as good in Tests and ODIs, as he will be in T20. McGrath can bowl well and take wickets in any version of the game. So will Warne. No one can be successful and reach the IPL level unless he has mastered the basic techniques as a batsman or a bowler. Can one really perform better in any other professional game – like football, tennis or golf – without having sound skills and abundant talent?

The same logic applies for money. Financial stability and its effect depends on individuals. There will be players who will be spoilt by it. But there will be others who will use it as an added incentive to do better. And it's the latter who will manage to stay at the top for longer periods. Has Tendulkar become a lesser batsman because he earns so much? Or Dhoni? Or Dravid? By contrast, there will always be a Kambli, or Karthik who will become slaves to the money.

Several young cricketers we spoke to replied almost in the same vein when asked about the negative impact of money. 'No serious player plays for money. Being paid well only pushes a cricketer to improve and become a better player. The rules that apply in any other profession are applicable in the case of sports.'

As we walked out of Gymkhana Grounds after meeting Sarvesh, we began to believe in such arguments. Despite his IPL success, Sarvesh still practices every morning and evening for a few hours each, if he is not playing a match. Money can have the same adverse impact as fame and recognition. All of them can ruin a player, but only if they get to his head. If that happens, then it doesn't matter whether you are an amateur or a professional.

However, there's another side to the IPL coin. Ashish Nehra, who played for Mumbai Indians seemed comfortable with the money that he had earned from the IPL.

After IPL, Nehra was close to signing a deal with Worcestershire as a replacement for Fidel Edwards, as the overseas professional, but the county's CEO Mark Newton issued a statement that stopped his pursuit as his wage demands were too high.

'The deal had been cleared with the Indian Cricket Board and we were expecting him (Nehra) to come and join us pretty much straightaway. But then he came back to us asking for more money and saying the deal started too soon. The IPL has changed everything. Prices have gone through the roof,' Newton said.

After the deal with the small, resource starved West Midlands club failed, Nehra claimed he was headed to the south coast to

Hampshire, one of the more ambitious counties desperate to break into English cricket's elite. (But even as the season drew to a close, his name didn't figure either in Hampshire's squad list or the scorecards).

When we met him, Nehra was busy on the phone making preparations for his UK visit, parents and brother in tow. He told his travel agent to look for seats in Virgin Atlantic, instead of Jet Airways or Indian Airlines even if the former cost a few thousand rupees more. We asked Nehra if the IPL has changed the fortunes of injury prone players of his ilk. After all, it was just a tournament that lasted less than fifty days and fast bowlers needed to turn up for just four overs, whereas the tougher examination of Test cricket included bowling in excess of twenty overs in a day.

Even if a player had a $100,000 IPL contract, he wouldn't earn half that money playing ten Tests in a year. 'If it was about money, I could get by fairly comfortably. Playing Ranji Trophy, domestic club cricket and a bit of county or English league cricket, I could make more than Rs 2,00,000 a month. I wanted to be back among the best. I wanted to play at the highest level again,' asserted Nehra.

Meanwhile, a Mr Patel called up from London to finalize Nehra's lodgings and travel in the UK. Maybe, Nehra was already financially secure; he claimed that he spent Rs 10 lakh on surgery and treatment of injuries over the last three years without any help from the BCCI. But, post IPL, life looked decidedly more prosperous. 'Don't worry about the rates. Get me a good apartment even if it costs 250 pounds a day,' he directed Patel.

So, we know one thing. Willy-nilly, IPL will change the game and the players forever. The future generation of cricketers will know and play the game differently from what our generation did. It could be good or bad for cricket. The bottom-line is that the gentleman's game will not be gentle, and only become manlier.

A Dada Goes,
One More Takes His Place

This is the height of power, fame and clout. The New York-based *Business Week* recently listed Lalit Modi as the 19th most powerful sports personality in the world. More important than the rank itself was the fact that Modi's position was four notches higher than Sachin Tendulkar, the master blaster (23rd). India's leading news magazine, *India Today,* included Modi in its list of 20 most powerful people in India. And former England captain, Mike Atherton, called him the most powerful man in cricket. There is no doubt that Modi has become the most talked-about – and talked-to – man in the world of cricket.

Depending on who you are talking to – his friend, foe, or beneficiary – you are likely to get different adjectives describing Modi. Ruthless, workaholic, demanding, and visionary are just some of those that you must have read. But we got funny responses when we asked a few people who had worked with him earlier in many of his television and entertainment-related ventures.

'I met him several times every day. And the one thing that I remember most was his shouting. He would shout at anyone, and everyone; for any, or no reason. He could shout at you because the sky was overcast, and not blue; or that the sun was shining on a summer afternoon; because his table was one degree more tilted than usual; or because his water was cold,' said one of them.

Another one piped in. 'I don't remember a single person in our office who hadn't been shouted at by Modi. When Lalit was in office, almost everyone could hear his outbursts at regular intervals. It could be because he had asked for something, and it wasn't done; or because he hadn't asked for something, and it still wasn't done. He would shout at you even if he hadn't asked for some work, and it was done.'

This group of people had another Modi memory. 'He would always wear white. I think he had some 100 white linen shirts because he always wore just white. The only time when he would be dressed differently was when he had to attend to his diplomatic duties. Since he was also the diplomatic head of Jamaica in India, he would wear formal suits or jackets on days he had to attend to those duties. On such days, his shining Mercedes would hail the country's flag.'

However, almost everyone agreed on one point. Modi got work done in record time. In fact, this 'Czar of Cricket', went a step further. He got his work done first, and thought about the legal and other implications later. Nothing could get in the way of an idea that had occurred to him. Unless, of course, if he himself failed to implement it, action it, or sell it to his superiors. This was apparent from the manner in which he pushed through IPL's second season despite the security concerns.

In his hurry, and in his obsession with his ideas, Modi would rub many people the wrong way. As someone, who had watched him closely as a boss, explained: 'Modi's business career is full of legal battles with partners and stakeholders. The reason, Modi would act before analyzing if his actions were consistent with existing contracts and agreements.' In his defense, Modi blamed his former partners for taking decisions that went against existing contractual obligations. The fact remains that Modi had sour relations with many of his business partners.

MODI AND ESPN

Consider the deal between Modi Entertainment Network (MEN) and ESPN in the 1990s (MEN was managed by Modi as part of the KK Modi group, which includes Godfrey Philips and ModiCare). According to an article by Atherton in Britain's *Daily Telegraph*, Modi's '... timing was spectacular. Indian cricket had been rejuvenated by the rebirth of its rivalry with Pakistan in 1978, by the 1983 World Cup victory, by the arrival of a cricketing superstar in Sachin Tendulkar, and most importantly in the 1990s, by the happy combination of double-digit economic growth, a burgeoning and consumer-crazy middle class and the proliferation of one-day internationals.

'Television did for Indian cricket what it did for English football: even in a country where running water can be hard to come by, where four-fifths of the population lives below the poverty line, 86 per cent list watching television as their main hobby.'

In an interview with *Indian Express*' Shekhar Gupta in February 2008, Modi said that the ESPN deal taught him a lot about television, cricket, and money.

'It (ESPN) hadn't launched, and when you're planning to launch ESPN and partner with them, the whole issue was, how do you make a sports channel work in India when there's no pay environment? If people don't pay for a channel, how can it survive? Everywhere else in the world, you have subscribers, who pay for a channel, and on that basis a channel survives.'

However, there was a positive side to this. 'When we talked to ESPN, we looked at all the genres of entertainment on television. We found that sports was the only genre that people were actually ready to pay for. When it came to a movie, they can watch tomorrow, they can watch it day after tomorrow, they can watch it on DVD, and they can watch it in cinema halls. But sports and matches are live and you're addicted to them. That's something people want to watch right there and then. They don't want to know the scores tomorrow; they don't want to know it from someone else.

'So we said, if we went and bought all the cricket rights in the world – at that time cricket rights weren't being sold by any of the boards; in fact boards were going to platforms like DD and begging them to put it on air – then people would pay to watch. But you need to have a system to collect the money and that's when our joint alliance with ESPN came in. We became their arm to make sure we set up a system.'

In another interview with *Tehelka*, Modi explained how he married television, cricket and money together through the ESPN deal. 'Cricket in India is a religion, ... Everybody wanted to watch it, but nobody was marketing it the right way. So we at ESPN, under Rupert Murdoch's nose, went ahead and bought the rights from the Indian Cricket Board, the English Cricket Board, Australia, New Zealand, West Indies, Sri Lanka. Murdoch got wind of it, and he bought South Africa and I think, Zimbabwe. But we had pretty much wrapped up the whole world. People, including BCCI's Dalmiya, told me, "You're foolish. You're paying us so much money." We had signed a contract for US$12 million, and Indian cricket had never seen such money in those days.'

Despite such claims, ESPN decided against the renewal of its five-year contract with MEN, which expired in September 2000. ESPN decided to set up an in-house distribution team. Media reports suggest that ESPN did this because it was exploring a tie-up with Murdoch's Star Sports. 'The Rupert Murdoch-owned Star TV Network, in fact, is keen to bundle its bouquet of channels with the two sports channel, ESPN and Star Sports,' said the then Star TV India CEO Peter Mukerjea. 'We are in discussions with ESPN to package the sports channels with Star Plus and other group channels,' reported *Indian Express*. In reaction to this news, a senior employee at MEN told the *Indian Express* that ' ... the decision to run their own distribution has been taken at the instance of Star TV. It has nothing to do with our performance, as ESPN is the highest priced channel and with the highest paid subscription and reach. It is doing better than Star Sports.' The same employee also added, ' ... we grew an adopted child. Because of the success of the child, the parents want it back.'

However, the buzz was that ESPN wasn't happy with MEN and Modi. The relationship between the two companies became more estranged when Modi went to court to force the sports channel to stick with MEN.

A small news item during the period stated: 'Modi Entertainment Network (MEN) claims to continue as the distributor for ESPN India's channels beyond the contract period of 30 September 2000, have been dismissed by the Supreme Court.... Monetary compensation claims by the Modis was also rejected by the court. On the other hand, a counter-claim by ESPN has been upheld and MEN has been directed to pay the sports network $2.4 million in compensation.'

MEN had similar disputes with other partners like the Walt Disney Company and Fashion TV (FTV).

Yet again, in retrospect, Modi talked of Disney in a positive manner. In an interview to *Financial Times* in April 2008, he said that the experience with Disney taught him how a modern entertainment conglomerate works. 'You release a movie. If the movie's successful, you build a television show around it, the television show sells more merchandise, then you have advertising revenue and it all piggybacks on the other.'

Modi told Shekhar Gupta that the arrangement with Disney 'went very well; extremely well, in fact. We had an agreement that they could buy us after ten years. We worked with them for ten years and they bought us out for 250 times of what we had invested.

'And in terms of the product too, actually. We made a lot of money. In that regard, it worked extremely well. It also gave me the foresight to understand all about marketing and licensing, it gave me a lot of insight into the field of sports, and into the licensing of other merchandise.'

But it was Disney, which dissolved the joint venture in 2003. Although Doug Miller, the then Senior VP and MD of Walt Disney Television International (Asia Pacific) said that 'we have had a productive business partnership with Modi Enterprises in India,' the truth was that Disney was peeved with MEN.

The bitterness intensified in October 2001, stated the *Hindu Business Line*, 'when Disney sought the (Indian) government's permission to set up a wholly owned subsidary for the launch of the Disney Channel in India. However, the Modis said that the clearance for the proposal was subject to Modi Enterprises giving a no-objection certificate. Modi Enterprises opposed Disney's proposal on the ground that the businesses of the existing joint venture company and the proposed wholly owned subsidiary were similar. Modi Enterprises' refusal to give the no-objection certificate forced Disney to put on hold its plans for launching the channel.' The point to remember here is that Modi's MEN only had the rights to market Disney programmes in India under the joint venture.

In case of the tie-up with FTV, Modi initially said, 'Our tie-up with FTV marks an active presence for FTV in India. We realize that the potential offered by FTV to the Indian fashion business is immense – it will be a window not only for showcasing Indian fashion, tradition and talent to the world, but a constant update of the international trends, styles, colours, etc for India.'

Reports in the media suggested that FTV was 'all set to provide the Indian fashion industry an added window into the international world of fashion. This will be done through up to 120 minutes of Indian programming ... every day. Other initiatives planned to create a presence for FTV away from the TV sets are FTV Cafés, FTV merchandise, shows and events.'

When the deal was announced, FTV CEO Rajan Kaaicker told the media that 'MEN's brief was not only to distribute the channel but also to work out ways to increase ad revenues (virtually non-existent at this juncture).' As to what were the initiatives that were being introduced to achieve this, Kaaicker could provide no details except to say that over the next quarter the results would be seen. Reacting to reports that the fashion channel was in the process of going pay, Kaaicker said 'it is not an option at all at this point. The focus at present is to promote the channel and increase ad revenues.'

However, controversy clouded the agreement almost from day one. B4U Television Network served a legal notice to FTV on breach of contract. According to B4U the 2001 agreement with MEN was not legal as FTV had signed a distribution and marketing deal with B4U, which ran till 2005. Speaking to Indiantelevision.com, and admitting that he had received a legal notice from B4U, Kaaicker stated, 'MEN had in no way violated any of the terms of its contract with the network,' and added that his lawyers would be filing a suitable response in due course.

Kaaicker felt that it was B4U that was in breach of the contract because MEN had honoured its part of the bargain in full and would continue to do so. Kaaicker added that 'FTV had terminated its agreement with B4U over two months ago and the approach for a deal had been initiated by FTV.'

Two years after the FTV-MEN contract, the two fought a bitter legal-cum-public battle. According to MEN, the dispute arose over its agreement with FTV 'for distribution, marketing, ad sales, advertising, merchandising and licensing for which Modi has a sole and exclusive agreement for India and the SAARC region.' The problem cropped up when FTV decided to transmit its channel on a 'free-to-air' basis, rather than remaining a paid one. FTV also entered into an ad sales and marketing partnership with Worldwide Channel.

This upset Modi, who claimed that the fundamental premise of its deal with FTV was that the channel 'must be encrypted, not free-to-air'. Modi got an interim order that 'directed FTV Paris to abide by its existing agreement with MEN.'

However, FTV alleged that MEN was not handling the channel properly. A meeting between Modi and FTV president Michel Adam in Paris on 5 May 2003 turned ugly. After the meeting FTV issued a statement that 'both parties agreed to disagree on further cooperation'. The fashion channel intensely fought the legal battle, and then said that the issue would be settled in a court in England as per the contractual arbitration clause.

Even while the case was being heard in Indian courts, FTV stopped its encrypted signal and went free-to-air. The decision was guided by the proposed CAS roll out in the four metros in India. It became the first private pay channel to do so at that time.

Finally, both sides claimed victory. FTV said that its channel's reach, viewership and financial state had improved after walking out of its contract with MEN. On its website, Modi's legal firm stated that 'the attempt of FTV to abandon the joint venture and set up an independent television channel and distribution network was injuncted by the Delhi High Court on a suit filed by us on behalf of Modi Entertainment. FTV was directed to continue its contract with Modi Entertainment leading to a settlement of the suit in favour of Modi.'

Later, several media reports suggested that the dispute between the two parties was far from over. 'FTV president Michel Adam says the channel is considering options to press criminal and civil charges against Modi Entertainment Network president, Lalit Modi, for fraud, extortion, harassment, copyright and trademark infringement in Europe.'

When Modi was associated with Ten Sports, there were regular pitched battles with DD. All the issues focused on whether it was a matter of 'national interest' to allow DD to telecast India-specific cricket matches even if Ten Sports or any other private network had bagged the original rights. In several cases, the Indian courts forced Ten Sports and MEN to share the rights with DD.

Though credit goes to Modi that he managed to establish contact with some of the unhappy and angry partners. In that sense, Modi is clearly an opportunist, who will fight someone if it suits him, or join hands with them if there is business to be done later. Not surprisingly, a Cricinfo short bio states that Modi is 'sharp, brash, ruthlessly ambitious, and admired and reviled in equal measure.'

MODI DOES A FULL CIRCLE

Consider what happened subsequently to his relationships with ESPN and FTV.

In a 2006 online piece, Ashok Ganguly wrote that 'viewers in India might have noticed tickers in the television channel, FTV India, advertising ticket sales for the recently-concluded Champions (Cricket) Trophy. Interested parties had to visit the BCCI website (www.bcci.tv) to buy tickets. I could not make sense of this connection between two vastly different entities, FTV and the BCCI.

'On one unimpressive day in Chennai, 9 December, when some of us guys were taking stock of stunning individuals on FTV, the camera panned towards the judges. Suddenly a very familiar face appeared onscreen! We realized that it was Lalit Modi, the vice president of the BCCI. Now what the hell was he doing adjudicating the Miss FTV Awards in Turkey?

'Soon his presence made sense. The BCCI was carrying ads on FTV, remember. And (there was) also one more important issue. Mr Modi, before his becoming the controversial public face of the BCCI, also ran Modi Entertainment Network (MEN), the company which gave Ten Sports and FTV to India. In 2003, FTV was preparing to file a civil criminal charge against Modi and Modi enterprises. The charge: MEN ... was selling the "Fashion Bars" idea to third parties without the consent of FTV. It had also accused MEN of collecting advance payments despite the fact that the agreement between them had been terminated.

'Things seemed to have become rosy post that situation, with Modi in Turkey on the invitation of Michel Adam, the FTV boss. How come there was no public press conference on a tie-up between FTV and BCCI? If there was a tie-up, money must have been exchanged. What happened in the intervening three years for Modi to be in the good books of FTV? There are a lot of unanswered questions, which we plan to look into.'

Similarly, ESPN-Star Sports and Modi seemed to have patched up when, in 2008, the former bagged the lucrative contract for exclusive global commercial rights for ten years for the Twenty20 Champions League. ESPN agreed to pay a mind-boggling $975 million ($900 million for the deal, and $75 million for marketing budget) in what was called the 'highest cricket tournament by value on a per game basis.' It beats the $918 million that the Sony Entertainment-World Sports Group combine paid for IPL's ten-year rights.

In a statement, ESPN-Star Sports MD Manu Sawhney said that 'this deal will cement our relationship with BCCI, Cricket Australia and Cricket South Africa, and we are committed to setting new benchmarks in broadcasting and distribution.' Modi, who conceptualized Champions League, said that 'this is the best commercial deal for Champions League.'

Although this story was slightly different, Modi had excellent relationship with DD before his court battles with the state-run broadcaster. A 2000 article in the *Indian Express* stated that 'Doordarshan has appointed Modi Entertainment Network to monitor whether cable operators are carrying at least two of its channels via satellite on prime band. "We have engaged Modi Entertainment to monitor carriage and quality of DD channels on cable networks and also ensure transmission of clarity signals of our channels up to the subscribers' end by cable operators," said a senior Doordarshan official.'

MODI THE OPPORTUNIST RISK-TAKER

Ever since childhood, Modi was always the wild card. He was one of the rich parents' brat, coming as he did from the once-powerful Modi family. He did what he pleased, and was always a willing participant in late-night parties. At some stage, his life itself became a never-ending party. He was born in 1963 and went to one of the oldest boarding schools in Asia – Bishop Cotton in north India.

Many of his friends and family members – none of whom wanted to be quoted as Modi is an influential figure and believed to be vengeful – said that he was a kind of black sheep of the family. He had no limits, no restrictions, no discipline. He did pretty much as he pleased, and when he wanted to. Like many of the rich kids, he went to the United States for college. 'His parents thought that studies may well help him settle down a bit.

But his parties and wild habits continued in America. In fact, he got into more trouble there,' said a family member.

According to an article in *Bloomberg*, 'While in a fraternity at Duke (University), Modi says, he and other students were charged with conspiracy to buy drugs. In a plea bargain, Modi pleaded guilty to a felony cocaine charge and two misdemeanours – assault and false imprisonment, according to court records.

'Modi had to pay a $10,000 fine and perform 300 hours of community service, the records show. Modi denies any wrongdoing.

'"There were no drugs actually there," Modi says. "There was no proof at all. You have the plea bargain system in the US. You just plea bargain and they charge you with a lesser crime."'

During the pre-IPL days, these charges came to haunt him. Modi kept denying and, after a while, the controversy died a natural death.

In the later days, Modi's altercations with his family increased further. For one, he really didn't fit into any of the companies being managed by his father, KK Modi. True, Lalit was on board of several group companies, but his interests were elsewhere. He was clearly bitten by the sports bug after having analyzed the success of basketball in the US.

Family sources say that his father was forced to start MEN to accommodate the wishes of his son despite being unsure about the viability of the television project. However, today everyone is all praise for Modi. More than that, they are scared of him. Even senior executives in the KK Modi Group refused to talk about him unless they had taken a clearance from the man himself. 'I have to check with Mr Lalit Modi,' said one. 'I don't think anyone will talk to you unless they have first informed Lalit Modi about it and taken his clearance,' said another.

However, what really changed the equations between Lalit Modi and his family, especially his mother, was his marriage. In hushed whispers, sources contend that Modi's mother was very unhappy since he married her best friend. But then, as we have been told repeatedly, love is blind and one can't accuse anyone of wrongdoing because of it.

Modi's wildness is also reflected in several of his other business ideas, whose flow never stops. He is a mine of ideas, whether workable and implementable or not. His brain is constantly churning out new ways to make money. Here are a few things that Modi planned to do in his pre-IPL avatar, except for the numerous tie-ups mentioned.

MEN's wholly-owned subsidiary, MEN Interactive Network, planned to foray into broadband technology, and proposed to provide basic and value-added Internet services via cable in India, under the brand name Modionline.net.

According to a published article, 'the group will spend approximately Rs 100 crore in capital expenditure and incur additional expenditure on upgrading existing infrastructure to adapt to the requirements of the new system ...

'Mr Deepak Nanda (project consultant) said that the company will leverage its expertise in the pay channel distribution business and subscriber management services to provide value-added infotainment across thirty-seven cities by 2002.

'The company will kick off the services from Pune where subscribers will be able to avail of it from December, Mr Ajith Pradhan, CEO, MiNET said.

'Mr Pradhan said that besides providing basic services of browsing, chat, e-mail and file transfer protocol, the company will also provide value-added services like video on demand, gaming, entertainment, education portals, web hosting, data storage and mining.... The company will target the home, SOHO and corporate segments for the services.'

In 2002, MEN joined the lottery bandwagon with Playwin, the global big boy in online lottery, to launch online lottery product. A *Business World* piece read: 'Reasons Playwin Infravest CEO RK Singh: "Gaming the world over is considered to be a part of entertainment ..." ... "Lotteries, per se, need high credibility," says Lalit Modi, chairman, Modi Enterprises. Now both players hope to create a marketing blitzkrieg around online lottery, which is a $125-billion business globally. Playwin will set up 5,000 and Modi 8,600 terminals across India.' The article concluded by saying that ' ... on paper, the plan appears sound. But then lottery is a game of chance.' As if chance and luck figured in Modi's vocabulary!

In addition, Pentamedia, the Chennai-based entertainment software major with a market capitalization of over Rs 3,000 crore at one time, 'entered into a 50:50 joint venture with MEN for production and marketing of television and Internet animation products. "The object behind the JV is to put together production resources of Pentamedia and distribution and marketing skills of MEN to tap the domestic as well as the global market," MEN Vice-Chairman Lalit K Modi said.'

Prior to IPL, Modi even thought about being the change driver for Indian football. In an interview with Goal.com, he admitted, 'I, through one of my companies made a joint proposal along with J League in Japan to work with the AIFF (All India Football Federation) to develop an inter-city football league in India. The proposal was initially green-lighted by Shri Priyaranjan Dasmunsi (AIFF president). But it failed to get acceptance from the AIFF. In fact, the general secretary Mr Takeo Hirata of J League and we had many meetings with the AIFF. Takeo even had a team come to India to take this forward.'

Then suddenly, between all these new ventures and tie-ups he walked into the vortex of Indian cricket.

MODI'S CRICKET KARMA

Cricket and sports has always been with Modi during his early life. As a child, Modi, played cricket like any other kid in India. He told *Tehelka* that 'I was a batsman but not very good at it.' After schooling in Shimla and Nainital, he studied sports management at Duke University in North Carolina (US). In America, he became interested in the business and entertainment of sports and began to understand the business models of American leagues in baseball and basketball.

It was the deal with ESPN that got him interested in cricket. This was when he strategized on how to really monetize cricket in India. He told *Indian Express'* Gupta that ESPN purchased cricketing rights from the BCCI for \$12 million for a five-year period. To enable the channel to become a paid one, Modi 'went about mapping the entire country to find out the cable operators, where they lived, how many subscribers they had. We learnt from the cigarette business. We in fact used the cycle salesmen who actually delivered cigarettes daily. We told them to map out where the antennae were coming from, who the cable operator was, got his address, got his phone number, asked them to find out how many subscribers he had. That took us about a year and a half ...'

In about nine months, ESPN became a paid channel. 'Our offices were stoned; a lot of our staff was beaten up. Slowly but surely after that, operators realized we were serious. They started to pay up, the cartelization broke up.'

By then, he claimed that he had realized the need for a cricket league in India. In an interview to *Outlook Business*, Modi said, 'India was the only country that didn't have the league culture, but had a huge cricket fan following. I always wanted a cricket league. I set up the Indian Cricket League thirteen years ago, and got it registered. I even got the BCCI's approval in 1995, but it was not open to getting foreign players to play in an Indian league.'

Modi was convinced that he had to become a cricket 'insider' to get things done. Especially in cricket since the BCCI was a monopolistic giant, and nothing could happen without its approval and blessings. In addition, he had to deal with Dalmiya, who ruled BCCI with an iron hand, a confident and arrogant swagger, and like his fiefdom for over two decades. In 1995, it was clear that the two didn't like each other too much, and even a leaf didn't move in BCCI without Dalmiya's nod. (In his younger days, Modi is rumoured to have boasted that 'he would put Dalmiya behind bars and throw away the key.')

Over time, Modi just loved to hate Dalmiya. He criticized the state of BCCI and its officials during Dalmiya's over two-decade reign. In one of his interviews, Modi said that 'while the television companies (read: ESPN) were professional, board members (of the BCCI and other associations) were spurred by other factors. When we dealt with the boards ... we always came across barriers ... There were vested interests, and within them, even more vested interests. There were roadblocks after roadblocks. Once they realized the value of rights, people wanted cuts.'

The moneymaking exercise, explained Modi, became standardized. 'One particular board ... would appoint an agent to market its rights. The agent would buy the rights for a million dollars ... Then he would sell it for $10 million to the broadcaster. The broadcaster would make $50 million on those rights. So, the value never came to the cricket board, only to the agent and broadcaster. If you analyze the last ten years' contracts of each and every board, if you look at the middlemen in each and every board, you'll find a revealing story.'

To decimate this arrangement, to become the moneybags himself, and to pursue his cricketing dreams, Modi planned his entry into Indian cricket administration through a side door, and with his identity hidden. He entered like a masked thief without anyone's knowledge. However, his first attempt – which was public – was a failure.

His stint with the Himachal Pradesh Cricket Association ended abruptly when he was asked by the state's chief minister to leave. Later, Modi said that he went quietly as 'we don't fight political powers'. In fact, in his second innings, he joined hands with political powers.

According to *Tehelka's* story on Modi, 'Mr Big Deal' (May 2006), 'Modi's entry into the BCCI through the Rajasthan Cricket Association, a decrepit body led by the Rungta family for over three decades, is legendary. ... a senior journalist says, "Yes, the Rungtas did nothing, but that doesn't justify the tactics he used there." Modi, however, maintains everything was done in the courts. "Fifty-seven members of the Rajasthan Cricket Association were members and peons of the Rungta household. There were thirty-two district associations and fifty-seven individual members – all of them Rungta's family members. So, I became a member.

I didn't give my full name because in those days my name would crop up and all of a sudden – pssch! – people would want to cut off my entry. So, I gave my name as Lalit Kumar ..." His application was accepted and he became a member. After he'd convinced everyone they were rubber stamps for the Rungtas, Modi says they changed sides and he took charge.'

For anyone, who understands the state of Indian cricket administration, this story sounds more anecdotal than real. No one can overthrow an administrator so easily. It would take a mix of politics, moneybags, tenacity and the ability to effect behind-the-scenes dealings. So, clearly by then, Modi had built up a sizeable clout to be able to oust Rungta.

This became evident as Modi's proximity to the former Rajasthan state's chief minister, Vasundhara Raje came out in the open. With the CM's support, Modi became the president of the state association.

One has to understand that Modi is no pushover; he never was. He hails from a family which, until not too long ago, was in the list of India's top ten business groups. Before the members of the Modi family fought with each other to death, and almost decimated their business empire, the family was ranked along with the Tatas, Birlas and Goenkas. Even today, the family has varied interests; Lalit's father owns cigarette giant, Godfrey Philips, along with other companies that his other sons manage.

So, Modi had enough opportunities and pedigree to cozy up to politicians. And politicians were willing to use him for their own vested interests. However, in recent times, Modi has made the right political choices. Rajasthan's Vasundhara Raje helped him become a state head. Then, in 2005, when the agriculture minister Sharad Pawar, who is among the most powerful and richest politician in the country, took on the might of Dalmiya in the controversial and intense tussle for BCCI's presidentship, Modi supported Pawar. That day changed Modi's fortunes – and Indian cricket – forever.

In retrospect, it seems that politics may also prove to be Modi's undoing. Once Vasundhara Raje's BJP lost the state election and her opponent party, Congress, came to power, Modi was on the back foot. Just weeks before IPL season two, there were police cases against Modi in Rajasthan, probably inspired by his bitter enemy, the Rungta camp.

Complaints were filed against Modi in Jaipur for various wrong doings. One of the allegations was that he had misused Rs 22 lakh out of Rs 7 crore that was granted to the Rajasthan Cricket Academy in 2007-08. Another charge was that he spent Rs 22 lakh during his visit to the West Indies in 2007.

Modi was accused of buying land in Rajasthan with fake documents. This was to prove his domicile in the state to be elected as the RCA head. The complaint said that his signature on the land deals were fake as he was not present in the state when they were signed. This new development put his re-election as the state cricket association president in jeopardy.

In response to these allegations, Modi said 'I have close to Rs 230 crore deals in the IPL. I don't even charge a single penny as TA/DA. Why should I get involved in such scams. The cricket establishment is with me but those who are not involved in cricket, who are not working are the ones agitating. They are all jealous people who are behind this.'

Modi blamed his predecessor Kishore Rungta of trying to benefit by the change in political regime in the state but said he was sure that would not happen. 'It's the Rungta faction which is trying to use politics, the change in regime in the state to their benefit. They think they can dictate terms like this. But I am sure Ashok Gehlot (the new chief minister) will understand and he won't let that happen. ... I have worked with multiple regimes in Rajasthan and many other states but I have had no problems ever.'

Not surprisingly, with reduced political clout, Modi lost the RCA elections in February 2009. The winner was a candidate backed by the Congress party. However, Modi put up a brave face and told the media that his inability to become the president of RCA wasn't going to affect his position at the BCCI.

True, since his political and cricketing godfather, Sharad Pawar still had clout within the BCCI. With his help, Modi became the youngest VP in BCCI and claims that he inculcated professionalism in a board that was ridden with corruption despite being the richest and maybe the most powerful cricket board in the world. (This was proved when the BCCI took on the might of ICC several times in the recent past.)

Professionalism – read giving top priority to commercial and business interests – became Modi's mantra. It was the same during his stay at the Rajasthan state association. According to the report published in *Tehelka*, Modi's 'maneuvers bordered on the Machiavellian: he persuaded corporate captains to pay over Rs 1 lakh for a single seat ... Then he acted decisively to improve the (state) team. Former captain Ajay Jadeja recounts that when Modi was told the state team lacked facilities, "he reacted within seconds and things started changing within minutes." Modi smiles when reminded of the incident. "In a constantly changing world, it is important to be on top of everything," he says.'

However, it is as vice president of BCCI that Modi's insightful commercial and sporting acumen came into the forefront. Wikipedia lists several deals that the BCCI has wrangled in the short tenure of Modi:

- Team Sponsorship deal for Team India with Sahara Group for four years - $103 million
- Team Apparel Sponsor deal for Team India with Nike for four years - $53 million
- Media rights deal with Nimbus for four years - $612 million
- Media rights for overseas matches with Zee for four years - $219 million
- BCCI sponsorship deal with WSG - $46 million
- IPL media rights deal with Sony - $1.26 billion
- IPL teams sale with parties - $723.6 million
- Web media rights - $50 million
- IPL title sponsorship and ground sponsors - $220 million

According to Atherton, in the four years prior to Modi's arrival at BCCI, the Board's income was estimated at $67 million. Modi told him that from the four-year cycle beginning January 2006, i.e. after his arrival, the Board's income has already crossed $1 billion. In the four-year period beginning January 2007, it would be $1.5 billion. As Atherton wrote: 'Modi has been ruthlessly efficient at exploiting BCCI property ... With technology changing at such a rapid pace, Modi plans to continue to exploit every available revenue stream.'

Modi's strong business acumen combined with BCCI's monopoly opened new doors for tie-ups and also allowed him to dictate terms. As Modi told *Tehelka*, 'I knew the ins and outs of production and sponsorship deals, I knew airtime prices, broadcasting prices, I knew the television companies' balance sheets inside out. I knew where they made their money and lost their money. So I called everybody in and played one against the other. It was as simple as that ... Right where you're sitting, I've had people come in and tell me to make the tender in a certain manner. But there are no deals. The deal is very simple: you come into the room and hand in your bid. If you win it, you take it. Same thing for team sponsorship. When I did the Nike deal, they were hungry. You have to build that hunger.'

In fact, Modi used the same transparent, but aggressive tactics in the pre-IPL days. Many would consider them manipulative and immoral. But for Modi, everything was fair in business and cricket, especially in the business of cricket.

One of the CEOs of the IPL teams told us that Modi and his other supporters personally contacted the various businessmen in India and abroad and cajoled, pushed, and even forced them to put in a bid for the team franchises. Despite this, they got a bleak response, although some big names like the two Ambani brothers did bid for the teams. Once, Modi had the names of the potential bidders, he started pitting one against the others. 'There were a whole lot of rumours flying around,' said this CEO.

For example, although the base price for each of the city's team was $50 million, someone whispered that Mukesh Ambani would bid over a $100 million for Mumbai Indians, which was duly passed to his brother, Anil. Now, Anil has an ongoing ego battle with his elder brother. So, the idea was that Anil may outbid his brother. This was duly passed on to Mukesh's camp with the hope that he would up his bid further.

In fact, when the final bids were opened, Anil still bid at the lowest possible price. But Mukesh went ahead and bid quite high compared to the other bidders.

Similarly, sources close to Modi contended that the IPL commissioner was clear about the telecast rights: he needed a bid of $1 billion. So, this was practically squeezed out of the Sony combine with a few creative calculations and permutations-combinations. Though Sony's actual bid was less than $1 billion, but with a few additions, it went up to $1.26 billion.

It was the same for everything. Modi usually had a target, or an objective and he would leave no stone unturned to get it. As far as IPL was concerned, he was a man possessed. Nothing could stop him, or deter him. The word 'no' did not exist in his dictionary.

After the unprecedented and huge success of IPL, Modi's ambitions have soared. So has his appetite to add more cricketing milestones to his credit.

To begin with, Modi wants to spend BCCI's newfound riches to improve the cricket infrastructure in India. A priority at the moment, Modi looks forward to making India's twenty-two international stadiums into 'state-of-the-art' facilities. In an interview with *Outlook Business*, he maintained that 'BCCI is a non-profit organization, and the money that comes in will obviously be used in the redevelopment of cricket infrastructure. We have already allocated Rs 1,000 crore before the (IPL) bidding for stadium renovations. Jaipur recently spent Rs 30 crore; Delhi and Hyderabad are undergoing renovations. We are even demolishing Wankhede Stadium in Mumbai to put up a world-class stadium.'

Most cricketers and fans would agree that this is a much-needed exercise. Atherton wrote that in Goa during one of the matches in season one, 'it transpired that thousands of spectators failed to gain access to the ground, despite holding tickets, because the stadium had minimal entry points for over forty thousand spectators. The Wankhede Stadium in Mumbai, the showcase stadium of Indian cricket, has disgraceful facilities for spectators.'

While talking to Atherton, Modi explained that the 'rejuvenation of domestic cricket in India is also high on his agenda ... The BCCI has promised to give the Indian players, international and domestic, 26 per cent of gross revenues, so they too will benefit.'

Slowly, over time, payments to players will also get linked to their performances, and not to what they achieved a few years ago. Franchises will pay as per demand-supply-performance equations.

Modi is also confident that IPL will become bigger than English football, and emerge as the best in entertainment programming on television. 'The English Premiership is a $10-billion business. We can surpass it in few years. If things go as planned, each franchise (in IPL) could be worth $5 billion,' he told *Outlook Business*.

'The IPL is an action-packed reality show. We are not pitching IPL against cricket; we are pitching it against the prime time (7-11 p.m.) of general entertainment channels. The more I hear about the entertainment plans of franchisees and what they are doing to create a fan following, I'm convinced that IPL is here to stay. To make a show a hit, one needs star attraction. We have cherry-picked the best players from across the world.'

To CNN, he said, 'we have added a lot of music to the games. I think it provides entertainment for the crowds and between breaks. People are able to lap it up and enjoy it – it's an evening out. A Bollywood movie is three hours. This is a three-hour function. A lot of good food and catering and popcorn and ice cream for the kids.'

In addition to the Champions League, whose first season has now been finalized for September 2009, IPL wants a second season in a year. Modi is determined to then take the T20 format to India's massive diasporas. 'He plans matches, as many as twenty-five per year, mainly against Pakistan, in neutral venues such as America, England, Dubai, Kuala Lumpur and United Arab Emirates, where India will play two matches against their great rivals ...

'His motivation, he says, is simply to take the game to an audience that only gets to see its team play on television; his critics point out that neutral venues allow the BCCI to keep the television revenues. He has already been in contact with the England and Wales Cricket Board to arrange matches against Pakistan at Lord's,' wrote Atherton.

However, added Atherton, such moves are 'likely to put Modi on a collision course with the International Cricket Council. India has already bared its teeth over the Future Tours Programme, which it thinks does not allow it maximum potential to exploit its home matches, and the Champions Trophy ... but which will benefit all nations rather than just one. The ICC is keen to allow some periods of rest within the Future Tours Programme, and it is likely to look unkindly on home boards which fill up every gap with more money-spinning opportunities,' felt Atherton.

At one level, this may be the best time for a man like Modi. The BCCI has enough commercial and cricket muscle to take on the ICC. In fact, this has happened several times in the recent past. The fact that Harbhajan Singh was let off during his verbal scuffle with Australia's Andrew Symonds during India's tour of Australia in 2007-08 was one indicator. Similarly, Modi has forced the ICC to accept a number of his decisions. Considering that the Indian Board is the highest revenue-generator in cricket, and has the largest viewing audience, it's probably time to shift the axis of cricket power more towards Asia.

As the bio on Cricinfo states: 'His (Modi's) abrasive and confrontationist approach – among other things, he accused the ICC of harbouring a neo-colonial bias – didn't win him many friends in international cricket, but both he and his adversaries are acutely aware of this: where there is money, there is muscle.'

With his tenacity, innovative ideas, a perfect understanding of the relationship between cricket and commercial interests, and his ability to bulldoze decisions, Modi is the right man for BCCI and world cricket. He has changed the game of cricket like no administrator has ever done before. And he has only just begun.

In just a few years, he has emerged as the new 'role model' for many Indians. Advertisers have begun to promote him. In many ways, Modi epitomizes the New Indian, who is ambitious, confident, brash and arrogant, and thinks he/she can conquer the world. Aided by changing and positive external factors and an inner urge to succeed, they wish to rewrite all the existing rules. They are the twenty-first century change drivers.

They know how to skip barriers, and side-step restrictions. They know how to be part of a system, and use it to suit their interests and objectives. No obstacles – whether legal or others – can stop them in their pursuit. They are plain and simple achievers. And the one person, although the comparison may sound a bit stretched, whose footsteps Modi may be following is the legendary Indian businessman, the late Dhirubhai Ambani.

Dhirubhai came from nowhere; Modi had a business pedigree. Dhirubhai was uneducated; Modi went to the best school and college. Father Ambani became the king in manufacturing; Modi chose to do that in the business of sports. That's probably where the differences end, and the numerous similarities begin.

The late Ambani showed Indians a new way of doing an age-old business by opting for polyester fiber, an entirely new fiber for making clothes instead of cotton. Polyester turned out to be the cheap man's fiber as cotton was too expensive. Polyester turned out to be the solution to clothe millions of poor people.

Modi did the same with telecast, sponsorship and media rights in Indian cricket. In the days when most people had no idea about such things, Modi realized that billions can be made of televized sponsorship rights. He changed the way people thought, especially within the BCCI, which worked like a non-thinking bureaucracy and power centre.

Dhirubhai's Reliance Industries used politics to sway a lot of critical decisions in its favour. Modi used politicians such as Vasundhara Raje and Sharad Pawar. In the case of Modi, his political proximity enabled him to get into a position where he could call the shots – at least in the case of IPL. The rest, as they say, is history, as Modi is today the most influential office bearer of the BCCI.

After their initial successes, both thought 'big' and 'globally'. Ambani set up some of the biggest refineries and petrochemical crackers. Modi did the same with inking the biggest contracts in the history of cricket sponsorship. The globe was their playground; India provided the launch pad, thanks to her burgeoning consumer base. Both catapulted India on to the global stage and pushed some of the existing players to the periphery.

In the process, they made powerful enemies. Dhirubhai fought open battles with the likes of tycoon Nusli Wadia, media baron, the late Ramnath Goenka of *Indian Express*, and former PM and FM VP Singh. Modi did the same with Dalmiya. They both won their respective wars and practically decimated their opponents. They were ruthless, believed in no-holds-barred fights, and used all means to win at any cost.

And yes, there were other differences between the two as well. While Dhirubhai gained most of his global respect towards the fag end of his career; Modi did it in his 40s. The latter did it within a decade; Dhirubhai took over two decades

However, success comes with its own set of disadvantages. Ambani's biggest trait was that he knew how to manage his rise, and continue to decimate his enemies. The late Dhirubhai never became arrogant enough to dismiss his detractors as weak. This is an area where Modi seems to be on a weak wicket. His loss in the RCA elections is a clear indicator that he underestimated his opponents. Similarly, one isn't sure what will happen to Modi once Sharad Pawar loses his clout in BCCI. Will other BCCI members continue to support Modi?

What's more important for Modi is that unrelated events are impacting his dream projects. The proposed Champions Trophy has already been postponed. After the attack on Sri Lankan players in Pakistan in March 2009, judging by the reactions of the various cricket boards and international players, the future of cricket in the subcontinent is being debated. So, the idea of a second IPL may be nipped in the bud.

In addition, foreign players are likely to refuse to play in India or Pakistan because of the attack on cricketers. Already a few New Zealanders (Jacob Oram) and Australians (Ricky Ponting) have expressed doubts about their participation in IPL's season two. Many more are likely to back out before the tournament starts on 18 April 2009. It will definitely take the sheen off Modi's IPL.

Modi has been forced to change the original schedule of matches in the season two due to security concerns – both because of the attack on the Sri Lankan team and the general elections in India. This too may lead to lesser eyeballs and stadium attendance after the shift of venue from India to South Africa.

It seems that Modi's fortunes, which were in his favour till recently, may be turning their back on him. From now on, Modi will have to tread a tough uphill path.

But no one can deny Modi's achievements. Like Dhirubhai, he is loved and hated, feared and reviled, and destroyed the existing system, created a new one, and then made it as rigid and non-transparent as the earlier ones.

One must finally remember that the two forever changed the way manufacturing and sports would be henceforth viewed by all and sundry.

Post Script: Modi, who loves to talk to the media, who was so obsessed with his coverage during the IPL days that he used to get a full bunch of clippings wherever his name was even mentioned once, refused to speak to us for the book.

His public relations person kept us hanging for weeks, and later said that Modi cannot talk to anyone since he and the BCCI are under a contract with a London-based publisher to remain silent as Modi is writing a book on IPL. It's a different matter that Modi gave a few interviews after that. Maybe Modi had become savvy enough to only talk to those who would write favourably about him. Maybe he was not sure about our book.

Or maybe Modi remembered that one of the co-authors had not written too favourably about the Modis, when the family members were fighting amongst themselves.

IPL or ICL
(Indian Controversial League)

It's ironical, but Lalit Modi's IPL dream was given a huge fillip by the early launch of the 'rebel' ICL. However, as IPL became much bigger than ICL, BCCI's T20 tournament was sarcastically dubbed as ICL – Indian Controversial League. A front-page article published in the *Indian Express* dubbed it as another version of IPL – Indian Parivar League. The reason: Right from the beginning, IPL was steeped in numerous controversies, allegations, un-gentlemanly incidents, rumours, and charges. The first of them was that Modi and BCCI had turned the new cricket league into some sort of a 'family' affair.

This seemed especially true of Rajasthan Royals, which won the league in its first season.

One of the co-promoters of Emerging Media, which owned the Jaipur team, was Suresh Chellaram, who happened to be Modi's brother-in-law. This was enough for tongues to start wagging: How could anyone claim that the bidding process for the franchisees was transparent if a close relative gets to own a team that won the finals? And shouldn't there have been a clause, like in any other bids, which states that 'related persons will not be allowed to take part in the auction process?'

Before we get into the answers to these questions, it is important to trace a brief history of the Chellarams since not much is known about the family in India.

The Chellaram family started its business in Nigeria in 1923, comprising trading in consumer goods. Chellarams Plc, the parent firm, was incorporated in 1947 and listed on the Nigerian stock exchange in 1978. According to its 2006 annual report, the company's turnover was just over Niara 8 billion, and the figure for the group was nearly Niara 9 billion. The gross profit for the same year was Niara 1.23 billion and Niara 1.32 billion, respectively. Suresh Chellaram, a British citizen, was listed as the firm's MD.

The annual report of the company states: 'The Distributive Trade Division has continued to be the core of our business accounting for about 75 per cent of the total turnover ...

'Subsequent to the year end, Chelltek Industries Limited commenced the manufacturing and assembling of Bicycles, Motorcycles and Two-wheelers ...

'The satchet-packing of Oldenburger powdered milk which is handled by the manufacturing division also recorded successes in its business during the financial year under review expanding its operations into packaging for other companies ...

'The Group equally expanded its activities in the property development market through the acquisition of a 50 per cent stake in Chellarams Nigeria Property Company Limited. The latter has acquired 2, Goriola Street, Victoria Island, Lagos for future development.'

A Google search shows that at least in the early 1990s, Suresh Chellaram was also involved in the import of cigarettes from London-based BAT, which has a huge stake in India's ITC.

In July 2008, a release by Reliance Money, part of the Anil Dhirubhai Ambani Group, announced 'its debut in Nigeria joining hands with Lagos-based Chellarams Plc, as a part of plans to expand its global footprint. This is the first initiative by an Indian broking and distribution company to offer a bouquet of financial products and services to retail investors in Nigeria, one of the largest financial markets in Africa also having the largest population in the region.'

In the press release, Suresh Chellaram stated, 'We are extremely happy to partner with Reliance Money and the new venture will be an efficient platform in Nigeria to transact Indian financial instruments. This partnership would also help us utilize their expertise by providing enhanced investment tools to a large section of population, who have not been able to use these services earlier.'

If Chellaram's connection with Rajasthan Royals was not enough, it transpired that another co-promoter, Manoj Badale had business, commercial and other links with Modi. According to an *Indian Express* investigation published before Modi lost RCA election in 2009, Badale '... runs the Cricket Star Academy in Jaipur. Modi is also president of the Rajasthan Cricket Association and the RCA's Future Cricket Academy, which has tied up with Emerging Media (owner of the Rajasthan Royals team) to launch Cricket Star T20, a televized nationwide talent hunt, of which former India coach Greg Chappell is also a part.'

The Jaipur twist became complex after Rajasthan Royals won in the first IPL season. Conspiracy theorists had a field day about how this was an almost-perfect ending to the tournament. David won against other 'Goliath' teams, Modi's and his friends' team won, and that too in an exciting last-ball finish.

There were other 'Modi' connections. 'One of the owners of Kings XI Punjab is Mohit Burman of the (Delhi-based) Dabur family. His brother Gaurav, who is based in UK, is Modi's step son-in-law,' revealed the *Indian Express* piece. When contacted, Burman told the newspaper that 'It's not just me alone, there are three other investors and naturally they won't be putting their money because I am related. The IPL is a good business opportunity and the relationship with Modi is a mere coincidence.' BCCI members too supported Modi as Niranjan Shah, the Board's secretary, told the *Indian Express* that 'there is no conflict of interest.'

But rumours that IPL franchise-searching process was a closed one refused to die as people realized that Vijay Mallya, chairman, UB Group and the owner of Bangalore Royal Challengers, was the vice president of the Karnataka State Cricket Association and also a member of BCCI's marketing committee. Similarly, N Srinivasan, vice chairman and MD of India Cements, the owner of Chennai Super Kings, was a treasurer of BCCI. Now what can be more obvious than that?

However, distancing himself from the controversy Srinivasan said, 'I'm BCCI's treasurer in my personal capacity, while it is India Cements, the company that owns Chennai Super Kings. There's no conflict of interest. Moreover, the franchise bids were opened in front of fifty people, and in any case there was day light between India Cements' bid of $91 million and the second-highest bidder (for the Chennai team).'

In retrospect, the bidding process does seem odd. Modi and his supporters claimed that they approached hundreds of potential investors to participate in the franchise bidding. Finally, four of the eight teams were owned by 'interested' parties. It seemed as if people were cajoled to make sure that there were enough bids to begin with, and for the whole process to be successful. As an outsider, one could sense that no stones were left unturned to ensure that.

In fact, it was surprising that IPL's first season was steeped in cricketing and non-cricketing controversies at regular intervals. It could be as inane as SRK's smoking, or the presence of scantily clad cheerleaders, as explosive as Harbhajan slapping Sreesanth or Mohammad Asif testing positive for dope, and as entertaining as the non-stop verbal altercations between Warne and Ganguly. It was as if even these were remote-controlled and deliberate.

We don't think any other tournament, or a series, has had so much of off-the-field action as IPL, apart from the infamous 'Bodyline' series between England and Australia or the Kerry Packer series. There was non-stop drama and excitement. And the media revelled as much in them as in the cricket.

SLAPPING THE GATE SHUT

'Slapgate' was obviously one incident, whose sound reverberated in all the cricket-playing countries for days. Not just because of its enormity, but also because the issue put to rest several misconceptions about international players and teams.

For many, who have played cricket at the lower club level, what Bhajji did was something we have done in some match or the other. It was the expression of raw animal emotions, when one is unable to control one's anger and frustrations. In addition, it was a facet about the simmering ambitions and win-at-any-cost traits that have become a part of every player. It epitomized the NewGen Indian, who thought he was the best among the best, and was out to prove it openly and brazenly.

Such emotions are generally curtailed, swept under the carpet, or simply capped at the international arena by a conspiracy of and gag orders on media, players and sports administrators. But since IPL, in many ways, had little control and restrictions – everyone was free to talk to anyone, including the media – there were no efforts to hide what happened at strategy meetings, dugouts, practice sessions and, of course, cocktail parties and night-out sessions. More important, the cameras were allowed to turn their roving, and 'peeping Tom' eyes on everything.

Everyone remembers what happened that day. After the match between Mumbai and Mohali, Bhajji, as he walked out of the ground after a defeat, slapped Sreesanth. It was only when television cameras saw a sobbing Sreesanth, and Mohali players and franchise owners trying to console him that the viewers realized that something had gone horribly wrong. In one loud whack, the slap had demolished several existing myths.

First, it proved that Indian players were not necessarily at the receiving end of verbal duels and sledging in international matches; at least not in recent times. In fact, Indian players have evolved as more aggressive players who initiate such encounters, rather than just react to them. This somewhat shocking realization changed the way audience viewed the controversial incidents involving the Australians during the Indian tour Down Under in 2007-08.

While Andrew Symonds' 'monkey' business was being debated and discussed, Bhajji was seen as the victim. Most Indians cheered when BCCI put pressure on ICC and Cricket Australia to prevent Bhajji from being penalized severely – BCCI even threatened to call off the tour, which would have had severe commercial repercussions on Cricket Australia. Indian fans raised the 'V' sign as Bhajji was almost exonerated while Indian players like Tendulkar supported the 'turbanotor'. They jeered when Symonds and Ricky Ponting got off lightly.

However, after 'Slapgate', the finger started pointing towards the Indian players. Experts said that several Indian players have been overtly aggressive and indisciplined in the past. If one were to make a list of the bad poster boys of Indian cricket, some of the obvious names would be Vinod Kambli, Sadanand Vishwanath, L Sivaramakrishnan, and Maninder Singh.

A simple boy from a middle-class family, Vinod Kambli's sudden rise to fame after donning the India cap became his tragic flaw. He lost his sense of balance, his collars went up and arrogance filled him up. The adulation, success, money, glamour and women distracted him and that marked the end of his cricketing career at the international level. Kambli was believed to be as talented as Sachin, but the former didn't keep up with the discipline that the game demands.

Vishwanath and Sivaramakrishnan were destroyed by bad habits, which reached a limit once they played for India. Their careers were cut short. Maninder Singh, former spinner of Team India was also embroiled in a public controversy pertaining to a suicide attempt and drug abuse.

There have been many other instances. Senior and respected players have been accused of late-night partying – even on days they were playing international matches – or even getting too embroiled with women during their several tours.

If one has to think of sheer laziness, one should take a long look at Yuvraj Singh, who is clearly the most exciting batsman that India has today. People who know him admit that he has exceptional skills and talent, but he will shun practice. 'If only he could have the determination and discipline, he could become greater than Sachin, Dravid, and Ganguly. But he doesn't believe in such things.'

Several reports in mainstream media highlighted how both Bhajji and Sreesanth were part of the new breed of arrogant and in-your-face Indian cricketers, whose aggression was not limited to opponents.

For instance, Sreesanth was reported as being aggressive during domestic matches and practice sessions, and with seniors like Tendulkar, Sehwag and, of course, Bhajji.

'A senior player narrates an incident during a training session in Chennai. "Sree bowled a couple of short balls to Sachin Tendulkar at the nets. Since Tendulkar wanted to work on his drive on that particular day, he asked him to bowl fuller. To everybody's surprise, Sree challenged Tendulkar to hit his bouncers. The next two short balls landed in the stands," he says,' reported the *Indian Express*.

The same article added, ' … after being hit for a boundary by Sehwag (during the 2006 Challenger Trophy), who was in the middle of a slump, Sreesanth reportedly told the opener that it would be better for India if he hits such shots in international cricket…. The jury is out on whether Sreesanth is an attention-seeking child, a misunderstood maverick or a bowler who feels his quirkiness will help him find a place in a country where only the batsmen are worshipped.'

Not that Bhajji is a saint. In fact, 'Harbhajan, who was reprimanded by the match referee in his first international outing, has a well-documented history of indiscipline on the field. Expelled from the National Cricket Academy (NCA) as a teenager, he has grown into a player whose emotions get the better of him far too often … Off the field, he was once involved in a scuffle with policemen at Guwahati when photographers were not allowed inside the team hotel.'

In comparison, the Australians came across as much better

human beings than the Indians during IPL's first season. As mentioned earlier, both Andrew Symonds, the villain of the 'monkey' business a few months ago, and Adam Gilchrist were praised by colleagues, coaches and managers. None of them had any problems either on or off the field. It was the Indians who got into problems more often.

Moreover, the Bhajji-slapping-Sree incident clearly made everyone realize that whether we accept it or not, cricket is no longer a gentleman's game. Given half-a-chance to express their feelings publicly, as was the case in IPL, cricketers would sledge, use unprintable language, and even slap their opponents. It didn't matter where they were from – India, Australia, Sri Lanka or West Indies.

This was the new form of cricket, where hustle was the name of the game. This was the extreme aggressive form of cricket, where international matches were played with same flair as club matches, where rules were meant to be broken and emotions could supersede the game.

MONEY, VICTORY, ANGER, FRUSTRATION

For us, there was a bigger question involved: Would internationalization of club cricket – which is what IPL has really achieved – lead to increased players' and fans' violence and anger on and off the field, just as is the case with football?

Look at a possible scenario in the near future. Ambitious, never-accept-defeat franchise owners such as Reliance Industries' Mukesh Ambani and UB Group's Vijay Mallya would want to win at any cost. Since IPL rules may allow transfer of players, these promoters could spend huge sums to buy the best players in a bid to build an undefeatable team. The same is true of English or Spanish football. The corollary is that players would be forced to perform even as they are being paid so much, or asked to leave. There will be enormous monetary pressure on players to deliver victories at any cost.

Ego will become an integral part of IPL, especially since it has franchise owners like SRK, a loud-mouthed entertainer, and chip-on-the-shoulder captains like Sourav Ganguly. With ego will come frustration, desperation and, finally, anger. These trends were already evident in the first season. How can we forget Mallya's outburst against his team's captain Dravid.

Newspaper reports indicated that Mallya wanted a different team than what was selected by Dravid and the original CEO, Charu Sharma. A *TOI* article quoted sources as saying that the liquor baron wanted Dhoni, Brendon McCullum and Robin Uthappa in his team. But all the three were vetoed by Dravid at the first auction. It's a different matter that if Mallya had bought these three players – who went for $1.5 million, $700,000 and $800,000, respectively – he would have had little money to spend to buy other players given the $5 million cap on each team.

Mallya, in fact, was so piqued with the performance of his team that he sacked Charu Sharma after just seven games of the tournament. Officially, Sharma resigned for 'personal reasons', but later he made it clear that he was asked to go. Actually, as a *TOI* report puts it: 'He had a ticket to ride, but barely three hours before the flight, the ticket was snatched away and so was his high-profile job…. "For details of why I was summarily dismissed from my duties, three hours before I was to board a flight to Kolkata for the next match, please contact representatives of the company," he (Charu Sharma) said.'

In another interview after he was sacked, Sharma added, 'Let us not forget that the team is still out there – on the road – doing its best, trying to improve match after match. The last thing they need is further distraction off the field. What they need is unconditional, genuine support. And that is what I continue to send them.' But Mallya was on a different plane. As he told reporters: '(What) I want from Rahul Dravid is to do the best for the team and to produce some good results for us because I don't think Dravid enjoys being at the bottom of the league tables, and certainly I don't.'

Then there were the altercations between 'King' Khan, and 'Prince of Kolkata' Ganguly. Problems between the owner and captain of Kolkata Knight Riders started in late May 2008. The

TOI reported that SRK was miffed with the performance of the team in the past few games, which had reduced the chances of it entering the semis. In fact, the article stated that there had been issues between the two from the start. 'Ganguly ... has not been too pleased with the team composition right from the beginning. The differences surfaced during the auction itself, with Sourav wanting more batsmen while the team management was keener on bowlers.

'The problems magnified when Coach John Buchanan was given more powers than the captain himself. To add fuel to the fire, SRK announced that the coach will make all the decisions for the team next year onwards, upsetting Ganguly in the bargain.

'Ganguly had apparently already begun to showing his discontent; he preferred to go back home after the last match rather than stay back for a press conference to announce Knight Riders' tie-up with a website. Said an insider, who was present at the event, "Shah Rukh did pass some caustic remarks saying, 'I thank all my teammates for being at the press conference but who can forget Dada who is missing from the event.'" The duo also had a spat when SRK was keen that his team field first in the last game against Chennai; Ganguly, however, preferred to bat first. Eventually, the Knight Riders lost by three runs on Duckworth-Lewis following a rain interruption.'

However, a few days later, before a crucial game, SRK sent a long SMS to his team, where he clarified that there were no problems between him and Dada, and that he had no angst with the team.

'Story time boys. I told you if you keep losing you have to bear with my long, boring msgs. This is your punishment. Many times I have made movies which don't do well. When I'm doing them, of course, I don't know they won't do well. The story is written by somebody else and I just do my bit as an actor. But I have a way of dealing with flop stories. I try my best to keep my character in the film at a level that it makes a failed story also special for me.

'I enjoy the work. I make jokes about the failure. And, of course, I feel awful about it too. So, right now, all of us have become part of a failed script. A bad IPL script. Let's try and keep our characters worthy of still looking back at this story and remembering it as a special story becos we all worked very hard at this. So, chin up and don't spoil yr character in the next two games. Let's go out with a bang and not a whimper. In films, we say u r only as good as yr last film. So let's make the whole world know how good we r in the last (maybe not) two games.

'Also, do ignore all this bit about Dada, me and John having issues. It's a normal thing. People like to hit you when u r down. So, we will be hit. No stress. It will make us stronger. The only way to avoid this is to win. That's one of the reasons why everybody likes to be a winner. On the other hand, the beauty of failure is that it brings people together. So, let's stick this out together. You know me well enuff to know I am not the kind of owner who has issues with the team cos of losses. I am too much of a sport myself to get beaten by defeats. Like you guys are. Like Dada and John…. So, head's up. Have a good match and let's make 200 runs tomorrow. This 150 seems to not work any more.'

Ganguly too dismissed talks of any differences with SRK or Buchanan. In an interview with the *Indian Express*, India's former captain said, 'Shah Rukh is not the kind of guy I could ever have any problems with. And it's the same with the other owners. I really don't know where these stories come from. But I'm pretty used to them. They don't bother me one bit. As for Buchanan, there is absolutely no problem between us. So the question of anyone taking sides does not arise. When a team loses a couple of matches, people start making up all these kind of stories.'

Whatever may be the real truth, we think that there can be no smoke without fire. And it's logical for us to assume that business and celebrity owners would have difficulty accepting a string of defeats – in business, entertainment or sports. So, their reaction seemed natural.

BUSINESS AS USUAL

In a couple of columns that Harsha Bhogle wrote for the *Indian Express*, he espoused similar views. 'It's players like (Dwayne) Bravo and (Shane) Watson that, I suspect, franchises will be looking for in the coming years; people who love playing cricket and give their adopted sides everything they have. It leads me to suspect that franchises might be a touch wary of superstars who are not too keen to belong. Certainly player attitude will be factored into player pricing from next year.'

In another column, he supported the team promoters openly. '... as cricket moves into the era of corporate management, and profitability, image and return on investment become key criteria, everybody will have to become accountable. At one level the cricketers are, because they get dropped if they don't score runs or take wickets and that will be extended to coaches and managers. It happens in football all the time.' In cases like IPL, cricket wasn't different from business.

But some of the senior players felt that there has to be a balance between corporate ends and cricketing realities, between earning profits and eyeing gaps on the field. The Sri Lankan opener-wicketkeeper, Kumar Sangakkara, in an interview said, 'In sport, there is a win-loss factor. But in the corporate and in the modern world there is demand for win-win. Corporates, at times, fail to understand that in sport you win sometimes, and· lose at others. But I think some day they will understand sport much better. The players too need to understand that it is the performance that counts, be it playing for a franchise or for country. If you don't perform, you will get dropped.'

Such discussions and debates are intensifying as IPL walks into its second season. Moreover, the repercussions will be reflected in the composition of the teams. Promoters and franchises will interfere more openly, and more frequently, in team composition as well as match strategies. We still don't know whether it will lead to more professionalism or not. Hopefully, cricket will become more like football and baseball, where coaches and experts have a greater say as winning becomes the overriding objective since corporates need to make money on their investment and strive for greater credibility and acceptance amongst their peers.

Several cricket experts we spoke to felt that IPL will also change the manner in which cricket has been monetized till now. Said one of them, who works for an organization that did think about buying an IPL team but backed out at the last minute.

'It has to be seen how the franchises and corporates respond over the next one or two years. Will they be willing to wait for three years, and willing to incur losses in this period before posting a gain? Will they want returns on investment to be instant? Will they look at IPL as an additional measure to enhance credibility and image? If you look at the eight franchisees, Reliance is clearly in IPL to enhance its brand(s). For SRK, it is a personal and individual brand-building exercise and the entire move is driven by commercial concerns. Preity Zinta gains more out of IPL than vice versa.

'One will have to see how commercialization needs drive these franchisees. For example, SRK was inundated with demands for complimentary tickets as people wanted to see him. Will he be able to monetize this in the near future? Apart from television money, every other revenue stream is a variable, be it sponsors, ticket sales, or merchandising. At the moment, all moves to drive city-based and club-based loyalties have failed. It hasn't worked. Neither has anyone made serious effort to drive merchandising. And I doubt if merchandising will ever take off in India. Similarly, in the case of cricket, you have players from across cities playing for a team or club. So, one can't expect any loyalty. If Rajasthan Royals wins the Cup, there can't be similar emotions like an Indo-Pak or an Indo-Australia.

'If I had a franchise for an IPL team, I would have done things differently. I would have tried to build a following for the T20 format or the city team at least a month before the tournament. I would have held a huge local T20 competition as a climax for the IPL league. I would have effectively used the star cricketers. For instance, I would have got well-known players to visit schools and other organizations and institutions. I would have held speaking programmes, where the players talked about their cricketing and other experiences. I would have organized after-dinner speeches, which were either by invitation or paid for. The cricketers could and should have been used better, and their presence should have been felt in the city before the league began. Much more could have been done instead of showcasing them at parties and at Page 3 events. The idea of commercial dinners – where people pay to sit in the same room as the cricket stars – will surely catch on in the future.'

He further added, 'For example, if I had Tendulkar in my team, I would have got him to speak to all my employees through video conferencing. He could have talked about how he became a leader, especially since our corporate philosophy is to build leaders in every area. I have got former Indian cricketers like K Srikkanth, Javagal Srinath and commentators like Harsha Bhogle for such corporate lectures. The international cricketers in my team would have done the same. It could have built a huge following, it could be successful. The international and national players could have been used to improve CSR dimensions. It need not just be the commercial exploitation of the cricketers; they could have been used to communicate key messages. For instance, Satyam took Gilly (Adam Gilchrist) to its 108 Ambulance Services, which receives 75,000 calls every day from across Andhra Pradesh. Gilly was thrilled and wanted to be a part of it.

'The franchisees should make an effort to bring the renowned cricketers out of their comfort zones, and out of their boxes. The cricketers have the power to reach the masses; they will be taken seriously by the masses. But these social efforts involving the cricketers should be sustained, and not just a one-off thing. So, the franchisees have to think in terms of five years, and learn and experiment along the way. The franchisees have to realize that IPL is a way to strengthen its presence in all the areas, and it is not just about winning or losing a match or a league.'

TO CHEER OR NOT TO CHEER

Apart from these crucial events, which would change the game completely, there were inane controversies that plagued IPL in its first season. They ranged from smoking, blackouts, and terrorist attacks to moral issues about letting scantily dressed cheerleaders into Indian living rooms.

SRK was shown smoking on television and the central health minister Anbumani Ramadoss could see smoke coming out of his ears. The lights went out at Kolkata's Eden Gardens, and there were conspiracy theories about who's responsible. Serial blasts in Jaipur scared the hell out of Shane Warne and other foreign members of Rajasthan Royals. They refused to play their next match at the venue, but only till security was beefed up and they were given assurances about their safety. But the most out-of-place issue was about the cheerleaders, who had become an integral part of any T20 match globally.

Prior to IPL, almost all the teams had chalked out exciting things around cheerleaders. Possibly, the best was done by Rajasthan Royals. Evgenia Guseva and eleven other Russian women stole the hearts of some fans, intrigued others, and angered some with their provocative costumes, lusty cheers, and wonderful dance steps. They were ogled at by almost every man who watched them. In a detailed piece, journalist Lehar Kala explored the minds and hearts of these women.

They didn't understand cricket at all; many of them had been cheerleaders in football matches in Russia. But then they slowly picked up. 'Now they are even familiar with the Royals' cricket team and are beginning to understand the god-like devotion that some of the team members inspire. "Shane Warne is the captain," smiles (Olga) Yarysheva.' It was Evgenia Guseva, who emerged as their leader, who explained to the girls how cricket was like baseball in many ways and worked out cues to start dancing when a boundary was hit. Anant Vyas, media spokesperson for Rajasthan Royals told Kala that 'When our side takes wickets, they have to be prodded to start.'

Guseva was learning hip-hop and salsa in Moscow and has

plans to start her own dance school. 'The rest of the troupe is equally multifaceted, with four of the girls in a university in Moscow, one studying to be a film director, and another a choreographer.' The money, Rs 25,000 per match, was good and the girls acknowledge it. According to them, it is 'almost 30 per cent more than what they would make at a football match in Russia. "More than money, we get exposure to something completely different, a new country and a new game," says Olga Yarysheva.'

However, in India, they had to face what most others have to quite everyday, '... occasionally, a Coke can would land precariously close to their podium. "There are some rowdy men but we don't mind the noise behind," says Victoria, another cheerleader.' In an interview with Kala, Piyush Inega of Inega Entertainment, which made arrangements for the Rajasthan Royals' cheerleaders, said that he was 'concerned about their safety in the country and he monitors their movements between matches. "They can't read the English newspapers so they don't know all the stuff that's being written about them," says Inega. "When they go out shopping, I have guards around."'

Though not many people were concerned about the predicament of the cheerleaders, many politicians were worried about their influence on the moral and ethical values of the traditional and conservative Indian society as their images were beamed every day into millions of homes. So, within a few days of IPL, the Maharashtra moral police brigade decided that enough was enough, and something needed to be done about this vulgar display of women on IPL's centre stage. It even thought about banning cheerleaders altogether. According to an *Indian Express* report, 'the issue was first raised in the state legislative council ... by BJP leader Nitin Gadkari. The Congress-NCP government, he said, should ban semi-naked women dancing in stadium just like it had banned dance bars in 2005.'

The minister of state for home in Maharashtra, Siddharam Mhetre felt that cheerleaders were 'obscene and simply vulgar. These are things meant for foreigners and not for us. Mothers and daughters watch these matches on television. It does not look nice.' Some of the state MLAs from various parties saw cheerleading as a part of 'western conspiracy' against Hindu civilization, and believed that it would lead to appointment of 'love gurus and sex gurus' in Indian schools.

Although these comments seem quite out-of-place, they had the desired effect. All the teams were told that their cheerleaders should wear more clothes if they were performing at the Navi Mumbai stadium. Maharashtra's chief minister tried to underplay the decision's significance by saying that the issue was being blown out of proportion. The fact was that it was accepted as a larger-than-life crisis by his government, which now felt propelled to act.

Navi Mumbai's police commissioner, Ramrao Wagh, too stood high on the moral platform. 'We have granted the cheerleaders performance licences and they are free to perform at the IPL match. However, this is provided their performance is not vulgar. If we find that they are indulging in vulgar dances, they'll be booked. Even courts have not come up with a strict definition of what is vulgar. However, senior police officers will be present at the spot, and if they perceive that the performance is vulgar, action will be taken,' he told the *Indian Express*.

Now, here's a police commissioner, who doesn't want to take any action against the crowd, which behaved badly with the cheerleaders. But he deputed senior police officers to judge whether the dancing was vulgar or not. In a city infested with crime and mafia, there were better things the officers could – and should – have done. Or maybe, they were more interested in the dances?

Taking lessons from Mumbai, many other teams backtracked on their decision to use cheerleaders. Delhi Daredevils were one of the teams to turn cowards. '... GMR, the franchisee of Delhi Daredevils, has decided to "do away" with cheerleaders for the rest of the IPL season. "The focus should be on cricket rather than entertainment. And the entertainment should be such that it blends with cricket," said a GMR official.

"'As time passed by, we realized cheerleaders were perhaps not needed. We want people to come and appreciate only cricket and nothing else. But I also hope that we can get them (cheerleaders) back for the next season. And hopefully, they will play a bigger role next time around. This time we didn't have much time to draw up an itinerary for them," said Shriram Ramdas, in-charge of entertainment at GMR.' How contradictory!

Such was the first season of IPL – full of contradictions. It was cricket yet not cricket. It was entertainment, yet not entertainment. It was fun, yet serious. It was commercial, yet skillful. It was corporatized, yet sports. It was smooth, yet controversial. It was deemed to be a failure, yet was a huge success. It was a success, but failure as cricket.

The King of Good Times

SCINTILLATING MOMENTS
FROM IPL SEASON ONE

Vijay Mallya put up a grand show of fireworks to kick-off the IPL in his den Bangalore that could rival glitzy events such as the Dubai Shopping festival, or the New Year's eve festivity at the Sydney Harbour Bridge. But just a few minutes after Mallya's crackers, New Zealander Brendon McCullum came to the party with some cricketing fireworks; his unbelievable 158 in 73 balls, with 13 sixes, ensured that the major event in the T20 era got off to a thrilling, entertaining, and exciting start.

Rahul Dravid and Wasim Jaffer, (the two would probably swear on the MCC coaching manual, if they ever had to testify in a court of cricket laws) walked out to open the Bangalore's innings in the same match, and managed an even more unbelievable 8 runs in the first 20 balls. Mallya's IPL campaign was doomed from that moment.

Mike 'Mr Cricket' Hussey didn't like it too much when his uncapped brother, David, was deemed more valuable at the IPL auction. So, he decided to vent his frustrations on the Kings XI bowlers by pummeling them for 116 in just 54 balls. Chennai

Super Kings made a tournament record of 240 runs establishing themselves as the big boys of IPL.

Virender Sehwag's 94 in 41 balls against Deccan Chargers was the first significant performance by an Indian player in IPL's season one. The icing on the cake was when he hit Andrew Symonds for 30 runs in one over. It was India versus Symonds all over again.

After almost ten matches, the lesser-known Indian youngsters had hardly done anything of note in IPL. Then Abhishek Nayar happened. Chasing a massive 206, and needing 62 off the last four overs with four wickets in hand against Chennai, Mumbai Indians' Nayar and Harbhajan Singh launched a scintillating counter-attack. Mumbai lost the match by three runs, but by the end Nayar had built a reputation.

It was the last over of the match and Rajasthan Royals needed 17 runs to win against Hyderabad. Having scored 117 off 53 balls earlier in the evening, Andrew Symonds was the man of the day for Deccan Chargers. Obviously, he could do no wrong, and so VVS tossed him the ball to bowl the final six deliveries. Symonds decided to trust his medium pace, rather than off spin, in this all-important final over. Pankaj Singh picked up three runs in the first two balls, and it was Warne versus Symonds.

Fourteen still needed from the last four balls. It was Aussie against Aussie. Facing each other were two players, who had performed many such turnarounds for Team Australia. But the challenge looked impossible even for the 'lucky' fat boy form St Kilda. Shane Warne drilled the third ball straight to the boundary for a four, and slogged the next one to cow-corner for a six. Ball Five: Warne stepped down, made some room, and played an inside-out drive that soared for yet another six. Match over, with one ball to spare. Of the 622 sixes in IPL, this one was probably the sweetest. Not only did Warne's miracle help his team manage the only 200-plus run chase, it was possibly at that moment that

Jaipur's team began to believe that their captain could win the tournament for them.

It was the kind of stuff that reality TV survives on. Bhajji slapped Sreesanth after Mumbai Indians lost to Kings XI. The turbanator was banned for the rest of the tournament and a few other matches, lost his Rs 3-crore contract. But the TRP ratings for IPL, and IPL-related programmes on 24-hour news channels soared.

It took a Gilchrist special, and the fastest century of the tournament for Hyderabad to register its first tournament win. Gilly smashed 109 of 48 balls with 10 sixes, in a match between two bottom-of-the-table teams. Shaun Pollock might have had only a few bad days over a decade long career, but it must have hit him badly to be smashed around the park for 33 runs in two overs.

Wasim Jaffer had a point or two to prove, especially as he was a part of the vocal minority of players who felt that they had got a raw financial deal at the first players' auction. Against Chennai, he scored a 50 with a strike rate of more than 100. And yes, Jaffer hit a six. Actually, not one but two. He hooked one to square leg. And then shocked everyone by stepping down the wicket a couple of paces and flicking Joginder Sharma for another one over mid-wicket.

Enters Swapnil Asnodkar. The pint-sized Goan was one of the many rabbits that Shane Warne pulled out of the 'Royals' hat. The game against Kolkata was Asnodkar's debut, and many were surprised that he was even selected for the squad. But his booming cover drives, exaggerated follow through, fierce cuts and compulsive hooking drew comparisons with the other pocket-dynamite Sri Lankan, Romesh Kaluwitharana and his 1996 exploits. Asnodkar scored a quickfire 60 off 34 balls, and added to the worries of other opponents, who were struggling for ways to figure out the Rajathan Royals' unknown commodities.

It was the day of debutants. After Asnodkar, it was the turn of the baby-faced Shaun Marsh, the nineteen-year old Western Australian and son of former Aussie opener Geoff Marsh. He scored 84 in 62 balls, playing silken drives, employing skill and grace rather than brute power to help Mohali beat the hapless Hyderabad.

Sohail Tanvir's slightly mysterious wrong-footed action and his ability to swing the ball fetched him the best ever T20 figures of 6-14 against Chennai. It was no surprise that this 'Royal' ended up as the highest wicket taker.

Not many knew of Manpreet Gony before the IPL. He had played only a handful of first class matches for his home state Punjab. A few IPL games later, he was seen as a useful and spirited seamer. But in the match against Delhi, where Chennai was chasing a stiff 188, Gony scored 13 in 5 balls including a big six off Shoaib Malik in the dying stages of the match. The blow not only helped his team win, it managed to grab the attention of India's ODI captain MS Dhoni. Gony was drafted into the India squad for Asia Cup immediately after the IPL.

L Balaji had a fairy-tale return to cricket. Not having played cricket for over a year due to a debilitating back injury, the Tamil Nadu medium pacer took little time to prove his worth as he scalped the wickets of Irfan Pathan, Piyush Chawla and VRV Singh to help Chennai finish with home and away wins over Mohali.

Sourav Ganguly finally came good with a 91 against Hyderabad.

Wasim Akram predicted that the temperamental quickie, Shoaib Akhtar would have a good IPL season. Not because Akhtar was in great rhythm or form, but Akram felt that the IPL cheergirls were exactly the fuel that would get the Rawalpindi Express chugging along. The former Pakistan skipper was not wrong. In a fiery spell of 4/11, Akhtar accounted for Sehwag and Gambhir, and Kolkata was able to defend its modest total of 133 against Delhi.

The pre-match buzz was about Sachin Tendulkar making his IPL start, but it was the other veteran and his opening partner, Sanath Jayasuriya who made the headlines. Barring McCullum's opening-day pyrotechnics, Jayasuriya's innings against Chennai was perhaps the most destructive in IPL. He made 114 in 48 balls out of the total of 158 that Mumbai Indians chased to win.

Deccan Chargers required 15 runs off the final over with four wickets in hand. Not an impossible task, but Delhi's leg spinner, Amit Mishra, made a short work of it by picking up a hat-trick in the last over becoming only the second bowler to achieve the feat in IPL.

Shaun Pollock wrecked Kolkata's top order, and SRK's dream of his team winning IPL. Pollock was back to his thrifty best, picking up three wickets for 12 runs as Kolkata was bowled out for 67, the lowest IPL total. The men in gold and black were effectively out of the tournament.

It was clear by Match 39 that Bangalore team was merely there to make up for the numbers. However, it was Dravid's turn to salvage personal pride and show his owners that he could play T20. He made a stroke-filled 75 in 36 balls, albeit in a losing cause against Rajasthan Royals.

The Mumbai Indians' game against Mohali Kings XI was probably the most thrilling match. Batting first, Kings XI made 189 helped by what was by now a routine Shaun Marsh half century. Tendulkar responded with a half century, and in the end, Mumbai needed two runs off the last ball. Tailender Yeligati hit the ball to Yuvraj Singh and dashed off for the single that would have tied the match and secured a semi final spot for

Mumbai. Yuvraj flung himself a'la Jonty Rhodes and ran Yeligati out. Singh celebrated the win as if he had beaten Australia in a World Cup final, prompting loud boos from the partisan Mumbai crowd.

The first semi-final between Jaipur and Delhi was all about Shane Watson. Watson played a middle-order cameo of 52 when Jaipur batted, and then accounted for Sehwag, Gautam Gambhir and Shikhar Dhawan, the big-scoring Delhi Daredevils top order, in his opening spell, reducing the rest of the match to a mere formality. Delhi Daredevils lost by a massive 105 runs.

Delhi Daredevils was not the only team gripped by stage fright in the semi-finals. The big hitting Kings XI Punjab was one of the hot favourites leading up to the semis, and Chennai Super Kings' early form seemed to be tapering off. Makhaya Ntini and Gony decimated the Kings XI line-up, reducing them to 40 for 5. Two spectacular catches from Muralidaran and Suresh Raina, and Ntini brilliantly running out Irfan Pathan also made it the finest fielding display in IPL. Chennai cruised to a nine-wicket win, chasing 113.

The final of the showpiece event seemed to be scripted by the best in Bollywood. Chasing a competitive 164, Rajasthan Royals needed 8 of the last six balls with captain Warne and Tanvir at the crease. Balaji conceded only two off the first three balls, and it looked to be slipping out of Jaipur's grasp – especially with Warne off strike. Then Balaji, the hat-trick hero for Chennai in an earlier match and who had used his slower balls very cleverly so far, bowled a wide outside the off stump. By the time keeper Parthiv Patel could collect the ball, the two batsmen crossed over for a single. That implied two runs without a legal delivery being bowled. And the rest was history.

Index

About the Authors

TR Vivek has been a business and features writer for nearly a decade with stints at leading publications such as *Economic Times, Business Today, Outlook* and *Business Standard*. At present, he is Business Editor of *Open*, a weekly newsmagazine. A sports nut, and a die-hard Ilayaraja and carnatic music fan, he lives with his wife and daughter in New Delhi.

With over twenty years in journalism, **Alam Srinivas** has worked for premier media organizations such as *India Today, The Times of India, Outlook* and *Business Today*. At present he is Executive Editor, *Money Today*. He has specialized in investigative pieces on the nexus between business and politics, and other forms of corporate corruption. Author of *Storms in the Sea Wind: Ambani Vs Ambani* also published by Roli Books, this is his third book.